International Perspectives of Crime Prevention 5

Contributions from the 6th Annual International Forum 2012 within the German Congress on Crime Prevention

Eds.

Marc Coester and Erich Marks

with contributions from:
Alexander Butchart, Marc Coester, Caroline L. Davey, Frederick Groeger-Roth, Burkhard Hasenpusch, Claudia Heinzelmann, Philipp Kuehl, Erich Marks, Melissa Marselle, Anja Meyer, Tina Silbernagl, Irvin Waller, Susanne Wolter, Andrew B. Wootton

Forum Verlag Godesberg GmbH 2013

Bibliographic information published by the Deutsche Nationalbibliothek

The Deutsche Nationalbibliothek lists this publication in the Deutsche Nationalbibliografie; detailed bibliographic data are available in the Internet at http://dnb.d-nb.de .

© Forum Verlag Godesberg GmbH,
Mönchengladbach.
All rights reserved.
Mönchengladbach 2013

Produced by: BoD - Books on Demand, Norderstedt
Printed in Germany

Print layout: Kathrin Geiß

Cover design: Konstantin Megas, Mönchengladbach

978-3-942865-17-3 (print)
978-3-942865-18-0 (ebook)

Content

Introduction 5

Lectures and Documents from the 6th Annual International Forum

ERICH MARKS
Opening of the 17th German Congress on Crime Prevention 2012 9

IRVIN WALLER
Balanced Investing in Proven Crime Prevention: A Crime Victim Right 21

CAROLINE L. DAVEY / ANDREW B. WOOTTON / MELISSA MARSELLE
Youth Design Against Crime
Enabling youth-led innovation in crime prevention 29

INTERNATIONAL CENTRE FOR THE PREVENTION OF CRIME (ICPC)
2012 International Report on Crime Prevention and Community Safety 53

TINA SILBERNAGL / PHILIPP KUEHL
Systemic approaches and collaborative action for realizing community
safety-experiences from South Africa 61

ALEXANDER BUTCHART
Preventing Violence: an Overview 75

GERMAN CONGRESS ON CRIME PREVENTION AND CONGRESS PARTNERS
Munich Declaration of the 17th German Congress on Crime Prevention 87

ERICH MARKS / MARC COESTER / FREDERICK GROEGER-ROTH /
BURKHARD HASENPUSCH / CLAUDIA HEINZELMANN / ANJA MEYER /
SUSANNE WOLTER
Some experiences by the Crime Prevention Council of Lower Saxony (CPC)
concerning quality-oriented and evidence-based prevention policies 91

Program of the 6th Annual International Forum 105

Authors 109

Introduction

The German Congress on Crime Prevention is an annual event that takes place since 1995 in different German cities and targets all areas of crime prevention: Administration, the health system, youth welfare, the judiciary, churches, local authorities, the media, politics, the police, crime prevention committees, projects, schools, organizations, associations and science. The desired effect is to present and strengthen crime prevention within a broad societal framework. Thus it contributes to crime reduction as well as to the prevention and the reduced risk of becoming a victim as well as fear of crime. The main objectives of the congress are:

1. Presenting and exchanging current and basic questions of crime prevention and its effectiveness.
2. Bringing together partners within the field of crime prevention.
3. Functioning as a forum for the practice, and fostering the exchange of experiences.
4. Helping to get contacts at an international level and to exchange information.
5. Discussing implementation strategies.
6. Developing and disseminating recommendations for practice, politics, administration and research.

Since its foundation the German Congress on Crime Prevention has been opened to an international audience with a growing number of non-German speaking participants joining. Because prevention is more than a national concern and should be focused internationally this step seemed crucial. Bringing together not only German scientists and practitioners but also international experts in crime prevention and therefore developing a transnational forum to foster the exchange of knowledge and experience constitutes the main focus of this approach. To give the international guests a discussion forum, the Annual International Forum within the German Congress on Crime Prevention was established in 2007. For non-German guests this event offers lectures in English language as well as other activities within the German Congress on Crime Prevention that are translated simultaneously. International guests are able to play an active role by presenting poster or displaying information within the exhibition.

Over the next few years we intend to develop this concept further. It is our wish to build an international forum for crime prevention that ensures a competent exchange of ideas, theories and applied approaches.

This fifth edition of "International Perspectives of Crime Prevention" includes the outcomes of the 6th Annual International Forum which took place within the 17th German Congress on Crime Prevention on the 16th and 17th of April 2012 in Munich and gathered together more than 4000 people from the field of crime prevention in Germany and worldwide. Along this congress the 2012 annual meeting of the Violence Prevention Alliance (VPA) took place. The VPA is a network of World Health Organization member states, international agencies and civil society organizations working to prevent violence. In two days over 50 international experts discussed the implementation of the new VPA structure, the Draft Plan of Action for the Global Campaign for Violence Prevention (GCVP) 2012-2020 and how the VPA can help implement this plan and gave updates on activities of the VPA project groups.

The articles from the 6th Annual International Forum come from Irvin Waller, Caroline L. Davey, Andrew B. Wootton and Melissa Marselle, the International Centre for the Prevention of Crime, Tina Silbernagl and Philipp Kuehl as well as Alexander Butchart which all presented important topics at the congress in Munich. Also included is the welcome address within the opening plenum of the German Congress on Crime Prevention by Erich Marks, the Munich Declaration (a summary of the congress outcome) as well as an outline of the Crime Prevention Council of Lower Saxony as one example of an institutionalized approach to crime prevention from Germany.

All articles in this book reflect worldwide views on crime prevention as well as the current status, discussion and research in crime prevention from different countries.

We hope to find a broad audience, interested in the upcoming events of the Annual International Forum as well as the German Congress on Crime Prevention. For more information please visit our website at http://www.gcocp.org.

Marc Coester and Erich Marks

Lectures and Documents from the 6th Annual International Forum

Erich Marks

"The only thing that is safe is that nothing is safe, that is why I am skeptical, to be on the safe side" [1]

- Opening of the 17th German Congress on Crime Prevention 2012 -

The main topic of the 17th German Congress on Crime Prevention is „Safe living in the city and the state". And if, according to Karl Valentin, nothing is really safe, it is even more important for us not only to be skeptical in general but also to critically discuss in an open and free society what type of security we would like to achieve, what is supposed to keep the society together and how we want to live tomorrow.

1. A very warm welcome to the German Congress on Crime Prevention 2012

I would like to welcome all participants and guests of the 17th German Congress on Crime Prevention at the International Congress Center Munich. I am glad that so many people have come and would like to particularly thank already now at the beginning of the congress all the people making this congress possible by their active participation as speakers, in the moderation and organization.

As in the previous years, many honorary guests have agreed to participate in the Munich congress. I would like to particularly welcome the representatives of this year's hosting organizer and also express deepest gratitude for the financial support of the 17th German Congress on Crime Prevention as well as for the pleasant joint preparation as regards the content and the organization of this year's congress

- Joachim **Herrmann**, Bavarian Minister of State of the Interior, at the same time representing the patron of the congress Minister-President Horst **Seehofer**
- Dr. Beate **Merk**, Bavarian Minister of State of Justice and Consumer Protection
- Christian **Ude**, Mayor of the state capital Munich and patron of the 17th German Congress on Crime Prevention
- Dr. Wilfried **Blume-Beyerle**, local government of the state capital Munich.

I would like to welcome the members of the Deutsche Bundestag

- Gabriele **Fograscher**, SPD fraction,
- Jerzy **Montag**, speaker for legal politics of the fraction Bündnis 90/Die Grünen,
- Hartfried **Wolff**, FDP fraction,

---

[1] A quotation assigned to Karl Valentin (1882-1948) according to http://www.karl-valentin.de/zitate/zitate-datenbank.htm (last searched for on 6.4.2012)

the members of the Bayerische Landtag

- Prof. Dr. Winfried **Bausback**, member of the CSU fraction,
- Prof. Dr. Peter Paul **Gantzer**, member of the SPD fraction,
- Petra L. **Guttenberger**, member of the CSU fraction,
- Angelika **Schorer**, member of the CSU fraction,
- Bernhard **Seidenath**, member of the CSU fraction,

the state ministers

- Ralf **Jäger**, Minster of the Interior and Municipal Matters of the state North-Rhine Westphalia,
- Thomas **Kutschaty**, Minister of Justice of the state North-Rhine Westphalia,
- Uwe **Schünemann**, Minister of the Interior and Sports of the state Lower Saxony,

the other speakers of the two plenary meetings

- Prof. Dr. Axel **Groenemeyer**, University of Dortmund,
- Prof. Dr. Hans-Jürgen **Kerner**, President of the foundation for crime prevention and help for misdemeanants,
- Dr. Wiebke **Steffen**, German Congress on Crime Prevention expert,
- Guilherme **Pinto**, President of the European Forum for Urban Security,
- Prof. Gerd **Neubeck**, head of company security of the Deutschen Bahn AG,
- Prof. Dr. Irvin **Waller**, University Ottawa,

the directors and presidents of central authorities and organizations operating nationwide and internationally

- Prof. Dr. Ilsu **Kim**, President of the Korean Institute for Criminology,
- Prof. Dr. Christian **Pfeiffer**, Director of the Criminological Research Institute Lower Saxony,
- Prof. Dr. Elisabeth **Pott**, Director of the Federal Agency for Health Education,
- Harald **Range**, Federal Public Prosecutor at the Federal Supreme Court,
- Johannes-Wilhelm **Rörig**, independent representative for questions of sexual child abuse,
- Prof. Dr. Dr. Armin **Schmidtke**, Chairman of the National Suicide Prevention Program for Germany,
- Jörg **Ziercke**, President of the Federal Office of Criminal Investigation and

the representatives of diplomatic agencies in the Federal Republic of Germany

- Envoy Dr. Corneliu **Alexandru**, Romania,
- Consul Aleksei **Semiletnikov**, Republic of Belarus,
- Ambassador Hassan **Tchonai Elimi**, Chad,
- First Counselor Ali Ramezan **Zadeh**, Islamic Republic of Iran.

I would like to cordially welcome the numerous municipal elected and leading representatives of public authorities and non-governmental organizations at the local, the state, the federal and the international level. I also would like to welcome by name from the large number of the national and international honorary guests Juma **Assiago**, Heike **Bartesch**, Jörg **Baumbach**, Dr. Paul **Beinhofer**, Dr. Karl-Heinz **Blümel**, Prof. Dr. Reinhard **Böttcher**, Peter **Dathe**, Johannes **De Haan**, Prof. Dr. Wolfgang **Eisenmenger**, Olga **Fleischmann**, Horst **Fleischmann**, Prof. Knut **Foeckler**, Dr. Isabell **Götz**, Prof. Dr. Christian **Grafl**, Prof. Dr. Wolf **Hammann**, Robert **Heimberger**, Christoph **Hillenbrand**, Mitchell **Jacobs**, Walter **Kimmelzwinger**, Waldemar **Kindler**, Marianne **Kölbin**, Robert **Kopp**, Rudolf **Kraus**, Dr. Martin **Kuhlmann**, Reinhard **Kunkel**, Gerold **Mahlmeister**, Alois **Mannichl**, Liliane **Matthes**, Hans-Jürgen **Memel**, Natalia **Mendler**, Johann **Rast**, Anton **Scherl**, Gerhard **Schlögl**, Mario **Schmidbauer**, Prof. Dr. Wilhelm **Schmidbauer**, Dr. Tina **Silbernagl**, Elisabeth **Schosser**, Wolfgang **Sommer**, Hubert **Steiger**, Harald **Strötgen**, Katrin **Stüllenberg**, Hermann **Vogelgsang**, Hans-Werner **Wargel**, Rolf **Werlitz**, Franz-Josef **Wilfling** and Prof. Siegfried **Willutzki**.

I would like to particularly welcome the present representatives of the sponsors of the 17th German Congress on Crime Prevention. Furthermore, I would like to welcome in particular all accredited journalists. Thank you very much in advance for your reporting in various media on the debates of the 17th German Congress on Crime Prevention and particularly on the wide range of prevention programs, practice initiatives and research projects.

2. Short supplement to the 16th German Congress on Crime Prevention 2011 in Oldenburg

The debates of the main topic of the German Congress on Crime Prevention 2011 in Oldenburg – "New Media Worlds – challenges for crime prevention" – showed the requirement and the prime qualitative and quantitative importance of crime-preventive discussions with and in the new media worlds. The Oldenburg statement, the impressive students' demonstration during the 16th German Congress on Crime Prevention and the published proposals and presentations were often picked up by the press and were frequently retrieved from the Internet documentation of the German Congress on Crime Prevention. And the topics as regards crime on the Internet and particularly suitable possibilities of crime prevention will certainly play an important role in the debates of the future German Congresses on Crime Prevention for some time. The German Congress on Crime Prevention itself consciously decided by means of various initiatives to make better use of the communication opportunities of the new media and to particularly develop better possibilities of provided information in the area of knowledge management:

The „small prevention search engine dpt-map"

The webpage „dpt-map" (www.dpt-map.de and www.pre-search.org), which has existed since the end of 2010, specifically searches for projects, measurements, institutions and persons from the field of work crime prevention. The sources for the search for key words and key terms are thematic data bases of accounted specialized organizations having already been published on the Internet.

At the beginning of „dpt-map" in October 2010, you could initially do research within 2,462 data records based on the webpages of the German Congress on Crime Prevention and the state prevention council Lower Saxony. Currently there are more than 3,800 records available. Further specialized organizations will be continuously included as partners. Any institution being interested in a partnership and linking of its data basis is expressly welcome.

The daily prevention news

Since July 2011 the German Congress on Crime Prevention has been publishing the current news particularly for the field of work of crime prevention and connected fields of prevention on a daily basis on its webpage www.praeventionstag.de. The daily prevention news informs on prevention events and relevant documents in the fields of prevention practice, prevention research and prevention politics. You may subscribe for or respectively make use of the daily prevention news in many ways: directly on the webpage of the German Congress on Crime Prevention, by way of a daily, weekly or monthly email, as RSS feed, via Twitter or on Facebook.

Presence with Facebook and Twitter

The presences of the German Congress on Crime Prevention with the online services Twitter and Facebook mainly providing and publishing the daily prevention news so far are still in the process of development.

The new App of the German Congress on Crime Prevention

Our new own app now also supports mobile retrieval of the knowledge documented on the Internet from the past sixteen German Congresses on Crime Prevention. This app of the German Congress on Crime Prevention, which was created by the company nanodesign, has been available for free download in the "iTunes App Store" under the keyword "prevention" since April 7, 2012. Some of the features of the German Congress on Crime Prevention app are:

- Offline research in the documentation archive of all congresses,
- Advanced search for persons and specialized organizations and
- Short information on the German Congress on Crime Prevention.

Updates for the app and content extensions will follow shortly.

Opening and closing plenum of the 17th German Congress on Crime Prevention live on the Internet

For several years the German Congress on Crime Prevention has also been publishing recordings from the opening and closing plenum of the annual congresses on its webpage. This offered additional information becomes more and more popular and is frequently used. The offered download of the opening speech of the 15th German Congress on Crime Prevention (2010) by Prof. Dr. Gerald Hüther in Berlin, for example, has already been used 20,000 times. For the first time the opening and the closing plenum of the 17th German Congress on Crime Prevention in Munich may also be watched live on the Internet. Due to the offered simultaneous interpreting the events may be watched in both languages German and English.

3. An overview of the congress

The 17th German Congress on Crime Prevention is organized as follows:

- Plenum at the beginning and the end of the congress
- 49 lectures about the main topic and further prevention topics
- 14 lectures in the 6. Annual International Forum AIF, each half in German and in English
- German Congress on Crime Prevention students university
- 54 short lectures (project spots)
- Exhibition including information stands, information trucks and special exhibitions with more than 200 participating organizations
- Poster session with 33 posters
- German Congress on Crime Prevention stage program with 10 activities
- Movie forum with 8 contributions
- Open special event „Security in public transportation and traffic"
- Special event by the Munich Initiative against Confidence Tricks (M.I.T.)
- 12 side events

In the run up for the congress more than 3,500 people were registered in total as congress participants and guests including more than 170 foreign participants from 34 countries.

4. The partners of the 17th German Congress on Crime Prevention

For the Munich congress the same is true once again: the German Congress on Crime Prevention lives on the excellent cooperation between many people and institutions! I would like to thank all partners and sponsors and their employees for their material and ideational support! In this connection I would like to point the detailed explanations of the respective working focus of the German Congress on Crime Prevention partners, printed in this year's congress catalogue, page 11 et. seq.

The 17th German Congress on Crime Prevention is supported by the Federal Ministry of Families, Senior Citizens, Women and Youth (BMFSFJ).

The partners of the congress 2012 are

as hosting event partners:

- State capital Munich
- Free state of Bavaria

as regular event partners:

- DBH-Bildungswerk (educational institute of the professional association for social work, criminal law and crime politics)
- Polizeiliche Kriminalprävention der Länder und des Bundes (Police crime prevention of the States and the Federal Government) (ProPK)
- Stiftung Deutsches Forum für Kriminalprävention (Foundation German Forum for Crime Prevention) (DFK)
- WEISSER RING e.V.

as main sponsor:

- Deutsche Bahn AG

as cooperation partners:

- Bundeszentrale für gesundheitliche Aufklärung (Federal Agency for Health Education) (BzgA)
- Bundeszentrale für politische Bildung (Federal Agency for Civic Education) (bpb)
- Bündnis für Demokratie und Toleranz (Alliance for democracy and tolerance)
- Deutsche Gesellschaft für internationale Zusammenarbeit (German Association for International Collaboration) (giz)
- Deutsche Sportjugend (German Youth Sport) (dsj)

- Deutscher Familiengerichtstag (German Family Court Day) (DFGT)
- Deutscher Jugendgerichtstag der DVJJ (German Youth Court Day of the DVJJ)
- Deutsches Jugendinstitut (German Youth Institute) (dji)
- Freiwillige Selbstkontrolle Multimedia-Diensteanbieter (voluntary self-control of multimedia service providers) (fsm)
- Kriminologisches Forschungsinstitut Niedersachsen (criminological research institute Lower Saxony) (KFN)
- proVal – Gesellschaft für sozialwissenschaftliche Analyse – Beratung – Evaluation (association for social-scientific analysis – advice – evaluation)
- Stiftung Kriminalprävention (Foundation Crime Prevention)

as international partners

- European Forum for Urban Security (EFUS)
- International Centre for the Prevention of Crime (ICPC)
- International Organization for Victim Assistance (IOVA)
- Korean Institute for Criminology (KIC)
- Violence Prevention Alliance of the World Health Organization (WHO)
- UN-HABITAT

as sponsors

- Deutsche Post DHL
- METRO GROUP
- Munich Re

as cooperating partners of the hosting event partners:

- Kreissparkasse
- MSF
- Münchener Verkehrsbetriebe MVG
- Stadtsparkasse München

5. The 6th Annual International Forum for Crime Prevention (AIF)

Within the framework of the 17th German Congress on Crime Prevention, the German Congress on Crime Prevention also organizes the 6th Annual International Forum for Crime Prevention (AIF). The 14 lectures will each be given half in German and half in English.

Lectures in English:

- „Sustaining and Mainstreaming Pre-crime Prevention: Glasgow, Bogotá and Alberta", Prof. Dr. Irvin Waller, University of Ottawa, Canada
- "Engaging young people in designing against crime", Dr. Caroline L. Davey & Andrew B. Wootton, University of Salford, United Kingdom
- Presentation of the International Report on Crime Prevention and Community Safety 2012, Dr. Paula Miraglia, International Centre for the Prevention of Crime ICPC, Montreal, Canada
- "Sexual Harassment, Sexual Assault and Women's Right to the City: Lessons from the Gender Inclusive Cities Programme", Dr. Sohail Husain, Analytica Consulting, Hampshire, United Kingdom
- "Building Safer and Inclusive Cities: The Experience of Delhi", Kalpana Viswanath, Delhi, India
- "Violence Prevention: Experiences from South Africa", Dr. Tina Silbernagl, GIZ South Africa and Partner from South Africa
- "Preventing violence: an overview", Dr. Alexander Butchart, World Health Organization (WHO), Genf, Switzerland.

Lectures in German:

- „Sicherheitsmanagement im öffentlichen Grund: Luzern auf dem Weg – ein Werkstattbericht!", Ursula Stämmer-Horst, Stadt Luzern, Schweiz
- „Trotz alledem: die Geschichte der Kriminalprävention in Kanada am Beispiel einer Gemeinde", Christiane Sadeler, Waterloo Region Crime Prevention Council (WRCPC), Canada
- „Lokale Gegebenheiten und Kriminalitätsgelegenheiten: Koreanische Perspektive der Haushaltsviktimisierung", Hark-Mo Daniel PARK & Dr. Seong-Hoon PARK, Korean Institute of Criminology (KIC), Seoul, Korea
- „Prävention und Gesundheitsförderung in der Partyszene: Mut oder Zumutung?", Dr. Katia Duscherer & Dr. Carlos Paulos, Centre de prévention des toxicomanies, Luxemburg, Angelika Kraus (Saarbrücken)
- „Sicherheitshaus - die Methodik des erweiterten Casemanagement und mehr", Julia Mölck, Kommune Alkmaar, Niederlande
- „Systemische Gewaltprävention – Methodischer Ansatz und praktische Erfahrungen", Anna Rau & Dr. Tina Silbernagl, Deutsche Gesellschaft für Internationale Zusammenarbeit (GIZ), Eschborn und Südafrika
- „Urbane Sicherheit 2025: Wie sich Schweizer Städte auf die Zukunft vorbereiten", Sybille Oetliker, Schweizerischer Städteverband & Dr. Tillmann Schulze, Ernst Basler + Partner AG, Schweiz.
- Violence Prevention Alliance der WHO zu Gast beim 17. DPT in München

Opening of the 17th German Congress on Crime Prevention 2012

Annual conference of the Violence Prevention Alliance (VPA) of the WHO

The annual conference 2012 of the Violence Prevention Alliance (VPA) of the WHO will take place as special event within the framework of the international forum of the 17th German Congress on Crime Prevention. Along with internal meetings of the members and delegates of the VPA, which the German Congress on Crime Prevention has been a member of for several years, information and a lecture are planned being open for all participants of the congress. The Violence Prevention Alliance (VPA) is a network of member states of the World Health Organization (WHO), international authorities and citizen organizations and has been operating since 2004. It has an evidence-based approach of public health care being focused on risk factors potentially leading to violence. In this context a broad range of cooperation of all concerned fields is intended. The members of the VPA work on spreading and realizing the recommendations of the "World report on violence and health" by the WHO (download of a German summary).

First publication of the "International Report on Crime Prevention and Community Safety 2012" by the ICPC

The International Centre for the Prevention of Crime (ICPC) is the only globally-operating non-governmental organization exclusively focusing on crime prevention and social security. Since its foundation in the year 1994, the ICPC has been working with the UN Organizations UN HABITAT and UNODC in a close partnership. Supporting the exchange of knowledge and experiences in international crime prevention and implementing relevant international research and counseling projects are part of its main tasks. From the Federal Republic of Germany, the German Congress on Crime Prevention has been a member of the ICPC since 2004 and has been actively participating in the leading committee since 2005. Since 2008 the ICPC has been publishing an International Report on Crime Prevention and Community Safety every two years. The first publication of this year's global report "International Report on Crime Prevention and Community Safety 2012" will take place within the framework of the forum of the 17th German Congress on Crime Prevention.

6. Sicherheit – Security – Safety

"Safe living in the city and the state" is naturally not just a matter of crime prevention in the narrower sense. More than ever urban security is a complex task involving several fields of work and departments with different goals and methodical procedures. And more than ever interdisciplinary discussion and department overlapping cooperation and coordination are essential conditions for the success of crime prevention strategies, of the employment of programs and projects.

The patrons of the 17th German Congress on Crime Prevention have already spoken hereto in their invitation greetings: For the Bavarian Minister-President Horst Seehofer "the security of the citizens is the duty of the government" and for the Munich

Mayor Christian Ude "safe living in the city and in the state is not a matter of course but the result of diverse efforts and endeavors by politics, authorities, institutions, facilities, associations and societies. The commitment and the dedication of every single citizen are required hereto."

In her – again – very impressive statement on the main topic of the 17th German Congress on Crime Prevention Dr. Wiebke Steffen writes summarized:

"Safe living in the city and the state" means much more than a life in external and internal security. Security also refers to – especially – the social and economic security and is thus both a complex social central theme and a fundamental human need.

Pledge and duty to provide security of the government

In the modern world governmental order is first of all and mainly responsible for ensuring the security of its citizens. The government is in charge of creating, maintaining and improving such conditions thus making physical, social and economic security, quality of life, foreseeability and planning possible for the citizens in the first place.

Crisis of the social state?

However, modern times are uncertain times. Fundamental social changes and current developments involve opportunities but also risks, and do not only "produce" winners but also losers. The social and welfare state belongs to the most important tools in order to reduce the consequences of disintegration, to balance social imbalances, to create social justice and to ensure the inner cohesion of society.

But this pledge and duty of the government to provide social security for its citizens seems to have become fragile; the social state seems to be in a crisis. Politics in Germany, however, still generally adheres to the principle of the social state as an essential guarantor of individual freedom, social justice and solidly living together.

Social justice – where is Germany's position?

Due to the welfare concerns, widely-spread insecurity as to the future and with satisfaction with life having been stagnating for years, this policy also corresponds to the expectations of the people, since the life situations and opportunities in Germany have further deteriorated during the last years: increasing social injustice, hardening of poverty, lack of equal opportunity in the educational system, clear integration deficits as to people with migration background, substantial regional differences as to the justice factors income, education and integration – without doubt Germany has a high backlog demand when it comes to social security.

Fair societies are better for everyone – conclusions for social prevention

Prevention of poverty plays a key role, if increased social justice is to be achieved: social participation and an autonomous life are difficult to realize in poverty. Therefore, politics must tackle the root of all problems, social injustice. Therewith the **social state** is required again: examples of success could be the welfare states of Northern Europe apparently being able to provide equal realization opportunities in their societies.

Additionally, the **cities and municipalities** must become the center of attention due to the substantial regional disparities and must be financially supported: effective prevention must be locally "made to measure" for each location.

Citizen engagement is an essential part of the creation of social justice, the living part of the social state. Citizen engagement is not only a part of the social capital of our society but also creates social capital and social cohesion and makes social participation possible.

Crime – a risk of modernization?

Social security and inner security are connected: on the one hand the perception of inner security embedded in social security, on the other hand increasing social inequality and injustice may lead to an increase of criminality and fear of crime.

However, this is surprisingly not the case in Germany: the total number of criminality registered by the police has been continuously declining for years and in the meantime also violent crimes. The load of criminality is declining for all age groups, and fear of crime is also not increasing but rather declining – even though fear of crime may be a metaphor for everything in connection with experiences and fear in the context of social changes.

Crime politics instead of social politics – from a social state to a punishment state?

The – positive – evaluations of the development of crime, fear of crime and prisoner rates and the question of increasing punishment within the justice system and among the people lead to the conclusion that in Germany shifting from a social-political to a crime-political processing of insecurity, poverty and exclusion has not occurred yet.

In Germany the social imbalances, insecurity and fear triggered by the reduction of the social state do not seem to have been leading to a security state substituting the lack of or fragile social services with crime politics.

Germany on the way to a prevention state – conclusions for crime prevention

Germany is on the way to become a prevention state – and crime politics is required to counteract. Risky aspects of crime prevention need to be avoided, which could advance further development of the prevention state, and instead its contributions as to reduction of social insecurity, its contribution to more social participation, integration and solidarity need to be focused on."

I hope that we will all have an informative, stimulating and creatively discursive 17th German Congress on Crime Prevention. Apparently we are even more required to communicate on our understanding, attitude and measurability of effective preventive acting, since an autonomous, happy life of the next generations is the overall goal of all preventive acting.

Irvin Waller

Balanced Investing in Proven Crime Prevention: A Crime Victim Right

The harm to victims from current levels of crime are unacceptable in the 21st century. We have the compelling and empirical evidence that prevention stops victimization from crime. We know that investing in proven prevention gives us a dividend of less crime but also of less costs to taxpayers.

But we are not applying this knowledge enough to reduce the number of victims. We must balance expenditures on reaction with prevention. We must shift government thinking and investment to guarantee the right to safety - a fundamental human right - for voters who are (potential) victims of crime.

What is balanced investing in proven crime prevention?

Our current expenditures on crime are not balanced. Whatever the rhetoric, they go overwhelmingly to reacting to emergency calls, then trying to catch, convict and incarcerate offenders.

If locking up those who violate the law contributed to safer societies, then the United States should be the safest country in the world." Horner Committee, 1993

In the USA, they are once again bigger and better at this than anyone else. The USA has taken the over-reliance and so over expenditures on mass incarceration to extremes holding one in four of all prisoners in the world for a country with only five per cent of the world's population.

Unfortunately, they are not better at stopping crime. Its rates of property crime are little different from countries such as Canada or England and Wales who have made moderate use of more police and prisons. While its murder rates is 200% higher than both of those countries.

If governments and so taxpayers are to pay on the basis of results in reducing crime, we would see a massive shift from traditional policing strategies and mass incarceration to smart problem oriented policing and targeted social crime prevention. I am going to highlight where those investments would provide a return of protecting crime victims and taxpayers.

I am also going to call for balanced investing – for instance matching every additional euro for standard policing, courts and corrections with a euro for prevention. I will also show how to make the shift from where we are now – for instance through the leadership of a crime reduction board.

Crime as harm to victims

In 1985, every government who was a member of the UN General Assembly agreed that resolution that recognised that crime is not just a violation of a national law but causes pain and suffering to victims. Today, we can measure that harm and know that it amounts to hundreds of billions of Euros for a country with the population of Germany.

In my recent book on Rights for Victims of Crime: Rebalancing Justice, I demonstrated that homicide and dangerous driving account for about a quarter of that harm in the USA but the less visible crimes of rape and childabuse remain so frequent that they are estimated each to cause as much pain and suffering. With a lower rate of murder in Germany, this would be even more true.

This means that our investments in effective prevention and smart policing must reduce fatal crimes such as murder and dangerous driving but also rape, child abuse, assault as well as property crime.

Smart Policing and Effective Prevention Reduce Crime

The World Health Organization reviewed the scientific studies on what prevents violence in 2002. It asserts that violence is preventable, not inevitable, and recommends investing significantly in proven and targeted pre-crime prevention and services for victims of crime. Mandela wrote the foreword.

I repeat violence is preventable, not inevitable. Little did he know that just ten years later a plethora of government agencies across the world provide living proof. The World Health Organization again in 2009 and now U.S. Department of Justice have scoured the world to provide even more. In my country, Public Safety Canada and the Public Health Agency of Canada – yes the public health agency - have selected best practices and made them publicly accessible.

These vital sources of hope for crime reduction are based on scientific studies that typically use random control trials to test empirically where the projects have worked. They also have a basis in "logic models", where programs are developed to tackle an empirically proven cause or risk factor, such as inconsistent parenting or dropping out of school. These causes have been established through a plethoria of longitudinal studies that follow-up thousands of young people from birth into their teenage years and beyond.

We also know that policing that is intelligence led can reduce prolific offending. Importantly, problem oriented policing strategies in collaboration with citizens and local agencies reduce many property crimes.

But despite their scientifically validated success, these effective prevention and smart policing practices have yet to be shared and implemented sufficiently to reduce significantly and nationally the costly harm to victims or limit the growth of the unsustainable costs of police, emergency care and prisons to taxpayers.

Fortunately, a growing number of "super cops" are lining up with the science, albeit with an emphasis on balancing tough-on-criminal and tough-on-cause approaches.

Bill Bratton stresses prevention, saying, "You cannot arrest your way out of [street violence]." Credited with reducing homicides in New York City in the 1990s through tough policing, Bratton knows what he is talking about. He was also chief of police in Boston, and Los Angeles.

Similarly, the chief of detectives for Glasgow, one of the U.K.'s most violent cities, got fed up investigating homicides. Looking for another option, he called in public health specialists, took knowledge from around the world and applied it locally, targeting gang violence.

My fellow countryman, Dale McFee, president of the Canadian Association of Chiefs of Police, is wasting no time to adapt these lessons to Canada, where they are very much needed.

Increasingly I hear these leading police executives and their organizations such as the International Association of Chiefs of Police calling for this innovation and for police leaders to argue for the investments in the agencies that can prevent crime and assist victims.

In my book, I have used examples of successful best practices and social science research knowledge to show that national and local governments could reduce the number of crime victims by 50 per cent or more by shifting from over-reliance on traditional policing and corrections to smart use of police and investments in effective prevention. I am going to highlight some of these for you.

We know that programs targeted to priority areas that address inconsistent parenting such Triple P, public health nurse visitations and enriched child care reduce both child abuse and teenage violence.

We know that programs that outreach to youth at risk such as mentoring or youth inclusion projects prevent juvenile offending. In the UK, the success of the youth inclusion projects in 72 areas lead to investments in double the number of projects.

We know that programs that analyse data from hospital emergency admissions to go to the roots of the violence prevent crime. We also know that programs that restrict access to other facilitators of violence such as knives or guns prevent crime.

In Winnipeg for instance, the number of victims of car thefts have been significantly reduced by an Auto Theft Suppression Strategy that combines smart enforcement, victim protection and pre-crime prevention. Since 2005, the investment of $50 million has been recovered with $40 million saved each year to taxpayers and likely much more in reduced harm to victims.

There are several other examples of collective efficacy. In Seattle as early as the 1970's, city hall hired outreach workers to create collective efficacy between neighbors and so reduce burglaries by 50% within three years.

In Glasgow, the Scottish government brought in public-health experts and oversaw the installation of programs to limit alcohol abuse, stop youth from carrying weapons, promote mentoring, improve bad parenting, and more. Five years later, these efforts have reduced rates of violent offending by 50 per cent among those engaging with the initiative.

Even the rampant rates of violence against women can be reduced. WHO has identified special courses in school that change male attitudes and so reduce violence against women. An innovative new curriculum in schools called the Fourth R: Relationship-Based Violence Prevention is being used more and more across Canada but could be used yet more to significantly reduce the number of women who are victims of violence.

We know from scientific evaluations of focused restorative justice programs that victims get more satisfaction and offenders recidivate less. The use of this knowledge is spreading these programs across the UK.

Return on Investment

In the early 1990's, the UK Audit Commission analysed the empirical data on projects tackling juvenile offending. Their conclusion was that investments had to be made before juveniles became offenders, because the costs of reacting and catching offenders were huge and very inefficient. Their report was poignantly called Misspent Youth.

Later in the 1990's, the Rand corporation did a similar analysis for adult offending in California. Their conclusion was similar but actually shows that a dollar invested in parent training or programs to help at risk youth stay in school will reduce crime seven times more efficiently than incarceration.

Now in the 2000's, the legislators in Washington State are provided with data on the cost benefits of a range of different interventions and prevention programs. These data measure the benefits separately for reductions in harm to victims and reductions in notional costs to policing and prisons.

In my book, I have used these data to extrapolate the return on investment in "effective violence prevention" over a ten year period for the equivalent of 10% of current expenditures on enforcement and criminal justice. I estimate the reduction at more than 50%.

Harnessing Knowledge to Prevent Crime

But the book is not just enabling legislators, taxpayers, voters and potential victims to understand the potential of prevention. It has led to real action. It has also coincided with the initiatives of WHO, Habitat and UNODC that propose similar actions.

These programs have to be directed by good governance strategies that are sustained, comprehensive and results oriented. These need a responsibility center at highest level, sustained investment in training, standards and capacity development as well as 3 year action plans with ten year vision. These must be multi-pronged (enforcement, design, social ...) and a portfolio of short and long term investments. They need to be multi-agency problem solving:

- Diagnosis, plan, implementation, evaluation
- Collaborative that brings together key agencies such as schools, social services,
- Engages public
- All orders of government – municipalities have key role to play but require financial and technical support from other orders of government
- Measuring outcomes/results independently of justice processes – e.g. using victimization surveys, surveys of violence against women, health data (death and injury), costs and consequences of crime

The United Nations knows that. But so does, Alberta who has a comprehensive, permanent and evidence based crime reduction and community safety strategy balancing smart enforcement, treatment programs and effective pre-crime prevention. This strategy is framed in terms of reducing the numbers of victims of crime and harm to victims. In March 2011, they held a provincial workshop on Community Mobilization that are available on the web and are examining ways to implement the recommendations from that workshop.

The government of the Province of Alberta has invested $500 million in new dollars over three years into a strategy that balances enforcement, treatment and prevention – the three pronged strategy. It is run by SafeCom which is a modern day responsibility centre that co-locates senior officials from five ministries and is mandated to follow a long term strategy to significantly reduce crime and prevent victimization over a ten year period. This strategy is expected to use surveys such as victimization surveys to measure performance.

Inspired in part by the European Forum for Urban Safety, a National Municipal Network for Community Safety has come together to pioneer municipal partnerships that (i) diagnose the causes of their local problems, (ii) plan sustainable, collaborative and evidence based solutions, (iii) implement those plans, and (iv) where possible evaluate and learn from the results.

Their on-going work follows in part the recommendations of the Safer Cities: Action Briefs for Municipal Stakeholders. These are a significant tool for cities to plan better and invest smartly. They are written for local political leaders and heads of agencies such as schools, policing, health and so on.

The action briefs build on both the empirical evidence and the pioneering efforts of many Canadian cities. One remarkable example is Waterloo Region whose executive director is here today and speaks German. Her council has shifted investment in prevention from 5% to 30%. Another example is my city – our capital Ottawa – whose strategy focuses on reducing youth violence, preventing violence against women and enhancing community safety.

Conclusion

The challenge to policy makers is to make the innovative shift from over-reliance on what is expensive and limited in success to a balance between smart law enforcement and smart investments in what reduces crime and violence. Increasingly, policy makers are making that shift because it protects taxpayers and potential crime victims.

The rights of citizens not to be victims of crime require federal, state and local governments to balance their investment in effective crime prevention and shift to smart policing. They need to get to know the results of scientific analyses of the causes of crime and the results of programs that have succeeded to prevent crime by crackling those causes. They can read this easily in Less Law, More Order.

In sum, we have the knowledge to reduce street violence, violence against women, child abuse and property crime. We can reduce gang violence, repeat offending and ultimately reduce the pressures on emergency and reactive systems.

We can achieve these through a combination of investments in effective prevention, that includes smart investment in early childhood, youth outreach services, changing the culture of violence, and restorative justice. These must be paralleled by action to use police resources more smartly by focussing more police time on controlling alcohol and other facilitators of violence such as knives and guns as well as reducing design opportunities and targeting prolific offenders. The police actions must also be partners with, and supporters of, agencies who can implement effective social prevention.

In my book, I provide you a budget to achieve these objectives that uses the equivalent of 5% of your current expenditure on reaction (police, courts and corrections) to invest in the effective crime prevention programs. It also calls for another 3% to invest in services and rights for victims of crime, which I have now explained in the sequel to Less Law, More Order called Rights for Victims of Crime have explained in much more compelling terms.

However, you will notice that I also call for the equivalent of 2% of the reactive budget to help police and municipalities retool as well as get the training and data that are needed. In the book, I have called for legislation to get the governance processes for all orders of government.

In closing, I want to leave you with some concrete ways to balance investing in prevention. Here, I have shown how to do this by matching every additional euro for standard policing, courts and corrections with a new euro for prevention. Whether overall budgets for police, courts and corrections are growing or decreasing, within 5 years 10% of those budgets must be added to be invested in smart policing and effective prevention.

The strategy for prevention must be led by a crime reduction board in every order of government so that the funds are guided to where they are needed. The boards must braid funds from different ministries, develop human capacity, ensure that the data is available and so on.

Less crime and violence means less harm to victims, less costs to taxpayers and relief from heavy workloads for police, lawyers and corrections. It means our municipal, provincial and federal taxes are not side tracked into reacting to crime but can be used to enhance the futures of your men, women and neighborhoods as well as for our economic and social prosperity.

For the harm done by the offender, he is responsible

For the harm done because we do not use the best knowledge when that is available to us, we are responsible

The time has to come to balance investment in effective crime prevention to protect (potential) victims from crime. Thank you for listening.

Further Reading

see www.irvinwaller.org (blog and twitter feed on preventing crime and victim services)

Waller, Irvin, Mehr Recht und Ordnung! – oder doch lieber weniger Kriminalität?, Mönchengladbach, Forum Verlag Godesberg, 2011, Burkhard Hasenpusch und Erich Marks, Herausgegeben im Auftrag des Deutschen Präventions (Translation of Less Law, More Order: The Truth about Reducing Crime into German)

Waller, Irvin, Rights for Victims of Crime: Rebalancing Justice, New York City, Rowman and Littlefield, December, 2010

See also

http://www.preventviolence.info/evidence_base.aspx (World Health Organization, Violence Prevention)

http://crimesolutions.gov/ (What works ...)

*Making Cities Safer: Action Briefs for Municipal Stakeholders (*http://irvinwaller.org/policy-adviser-effective-policies*)*

Caroline L. Davey / Andrew B. Wootton / Melissa Marselle

Youth Design Against Crime

Enabling youth-led innovation in crime prevention

SUMMARY

Young people are commonly considered a source of problems, especially in relation to issues of insecurity in the public realm of towns and cities. In the UK, young people are increasingly accused of acting anti-socially and generating feelings of insecurity in other users. This paper describes a programme called *Youth Design Against Crime (YDAC)*, developed by the *Design Against Crime Solution Centre* at the University of Salford (UK) in partnership with a UK young people's charity, Catch22. YDAC engages with young people considered 'at risk of offending' and challenges them to address problems in their neighbourhoods using a process of research and design to help generate innovative and evidence-based solutions. This paper briefly outlines approaches to dealing with 'problems' associated with young people, and details the structure of the YDAC programme. It presents in some detail findings from a process evaluation begun in 2011 of five YDAC projects. This indicates the value of the YDAC design challenge in improving young people's confidence, knowledge, qualifications and skills, and fostering better relationships with adult participants, including local police. Teams of young people developed creative solutions to local crime problems, and were able to convince stakeholders involved in policing, community safety and urban planning of the value of their ideas. While the resulting changes in attitudes and skills may help divert young people away from antisocial and offending behaviour, YDAC also confronts preconceptions of adult participants—challenging stereotypes of young people, and demonstrating the value of engaging rather than excluding young people in society.

1.0 INTRODUCTION

1.1 What is Design Against Crime?

Design and innovation research at the University of Salford focuses on the role of design in crime prevention and the use of 'design thinking' to address issues affecting people's quality of life. Interest in the role of design in crime prevention dates back to Salford's participation in a research programme entitled *"Design Against Crime"* (1999 to 2002), which was funded by the UK Home Office and Design Council. Design Against Crime aimed to embed crime prevention into design education and professional practice, and included: (a) a project to teach school children about solving crime issues as part of the Design & Technology curriculum; (b) a competition that challenged design students to apply their creative talents to solving crime and related social issues; (c) case studies; and (d) professional development for design professionals (www.designagainstcrime.org).

In 2003, the *Design Against Crime Solution Centre* was established at the University of Salford—a unique partnership with Greater Manchester Police (UK) and DSP-groep (NL). The Solution Centre has delivered consortium projects on design-led crime prevention, social responsibility and sustainability, including four EU-funded *Design Against Crime* projects. The Solution Centre recently completed the EU-funded *Planning Urban Security* (PLuS) research project, led by the German Landeskriminalamt (state CID) in Lower Saxony.

The Solution Centre is innovative in its use of design to engage stakeholders, develop and communicate conceptual models and conceive approaches suited to addressing the concerns of citizens in the 21st century. The centre adopts a holistic, human-centred design approach, generating innovative solutions from a combination of creative thinking and a sound understanding of different stakeholder needs and requirements (Wootton & Davey, 2003, 2005, 2012). Human-centred design focuses on the human participants in a system, but goes beyond just physical ergonomics. Formal roles and informal (social) roles are considered, including behaviours, goals, motivations and aspirations. Relationships between different parts of the system being examined are taken into account. Good design solutions meet and resolve conflicting priorities and needs, and are suited to the specific context—including cultural norms, physical environment, systems of management and user services.

The *Design Against Crime* approach integrates consideration of crime and anti-social behaviour within the creative design process, involving research, idea generation and evaluation (Design Council, 2003, 2011; Wootton & Davey, 2003, 2005, 2012). More recent projects have supported a range of stakeholders in their efforts to address crime issues and integrate crime prevention into design, planning and management of urban environments (see www.plus.eu). Design-led crime prevention recognises that security is just one of a range of objectives. Priorities therefore have to be identified and trade-offs made where necessary. Crime prevention is a component of *Socially Responsible Design*, where design is used to help achieve social and environmental goals such as fair trade, equality, health and wellbeing (Davey *et al,* 2005; Davey *et al,* forthcoming).

1.2 Youth Design Against Crime

This paper is based on the authors' presentation delivered at the 2012 *Deutsche Präventionstag* on *Youth Design Against Crime* (YDAC)—a programme to engage young people in design-led crime prevention, developed by the *Design Against Crime Solution Centre* and UK young people's charity Catch22. Supported by youth workers and teachers, and mentored by local police officers, multiple teams of up to nine young people are challenged to address issues of crime and community safety in their neighbourhoods. The ideas generated are presented to senior local stakeholders, from agencies such as the police, planning authority and local council. YDAC is aimed at young people who have come to the attention of school and/or police authorities due to behavioural problems, and may be excluded from school and following an alternative curriculum. It is the first Design Against Crime project to engage young people at risk of offending in developing ideas to solve crime problems.

Previous papers on YDAC are aimed at design researchers and professionals (Wootton et al, 2011; Davey & Wootton, 2012). In contrast, this paper is targeted at authorities responsible for the management and safety of the public domain, and for tackling issues related to young people and deprived communities—including crime prevention experts, city planners and social services professionals. The authors present in detail findings from an ongoing evaluation into the impact of YDAC.

2.0 THE PROBLEM

2.1 Feelings of insecurity

In the UK, young people tend to be portrayed by the media, politicians and policymakers as a source of problems rather than of solutions (Waiton, 2006; Day et al, 2011; Fionda, 2005). Within the public realm, young people are considered threatening by some social groups, and feelings of insecurity may deter users from making use of public space and facilities. Fear and isolation amongst citizens are factors that damage wellbeing and undermine quality of life (Davey & Wootton, forthcoming). According to Fionda (2005, p.27) such attitudes may be linked to perceptions of childhood. The author suggests that children who misbehave are typically demonised and feared because they challenge adult social identity and the prevailing social order—which is considered 'stable'. Of course, concern about the non-conformity of young people to adult social norms of 'good behaviour', is not new.

"Children today are tyrants. They contradict their parents, gobble their food, and tyrannise their teachers."

Socrates (469–399 BC)

2.2 Crime and young people

The link between young people and delinquency is not merely a social construction, however. When we look at the scientific studies, evidence supports the view that young people—especially young males—are more at risk of committing criminal offences or engaging in anti-social behaviour. However, criminal activity tends to be concentrated around property crime, rather than violent crime. In general, the risk of offending peaks between early adolescence and the mid-20s, and thereafter declines (Farrington, 1986; McVie, 2005). We do not know whether the incidence of anti-social behaviour involving young people has increased because the term is highly subjective and UK legislation is relatively new. There is no evidence that offending levels have increased amongst young people, and crime levels across Europe have fallen (van Dijk et al, 2007). Fionda (2005) sums up by saying that:

"The problem consists predominantly of young men aged over 14 who commit property offences, occasionally persistently, and rarely commit violent or sexual offences. Overall youth crime has not significantly increased in the last two decades, some figures even suggest it has fallen."

Fionda (2005) p. 68.

We should not only consider the evidence identifying young people as perpetrators of crime. Research also reveals the above average victimisation of young people. Evidence shows that young people aged between 16 and 24 are more likely to be victims of crime than other age groups (Flatley *et al*, 2010). In England & Wales, the 2006 Offending, Crime and Justice Survey showed that just over a quarter (26%) of young people aged between 10 and 25 were a victim of either personal theft or of violent assault in the previous 12 months (Roe & Asche, 2008).

2.3 Causes of crime

Factors that are linked to offending and anti-social behaviour by young people include neglect, violence and abuse in childhood, as well as living in a low income family, with a history of unemployment. In terms of attitudes and behaviours, offenders are prone to negative beliefs and emotions, such as low self-control, anger, hate and distrust of others. They seek the immediate rewards that criminal activities appear to offer, rather than longer term life goals, and adopt a confrontational style that may mitigate against educational and career success (Burt *et al*, 2006).

Researchers have attributed bad behaviour amongst young people to lack of self-esteem. Lack of self esteem is especially common amongst those from deprived backgrounds (Lo *et al*, 2011). To feel better about themselves, young people may seek to impress their peers by acting rudely or aggressively in relation to those in positions of authority i.e. teachers at schools (*ibid.*). Anti-social behaviour may indicate a risk of offending for some young people, and early intervention is therefore recommended:

"In some cases, early intervention that targets young people involved in anti-social behaviour may help to reduce the likelihood of offending later on."

Hales et al (2009) p. i.

Hales *et al* (2009) conclude that family, peer group and school factors are important influences on the behaviour trajectories of young people during their teenage years. For this reason, interventions with families and schools are—and should be—the focus for intervention. Hales *et al* goes on to propose that interventions might disrupt the spread of offending amongst peer groups.

"The significance of peer groups, whether siblings or friends, as an influence supports previous findings emphasising co-offending as a feature of youth crime and raises the question of whether it would be possible to intervene to disrupt the spread of offending between peers."

Hales et al (2009) p. i

3.0 COMMON SOLUTIONS IN THE UK

In the UK, guidance on Crime Prevention Through Environmental Design (CPTED) recommends that designers of urban environments seek to understand the needs of different stakeholder groups, and address potentially conflicting requirements of urban environments. It also highlights the benefit of consulting with young people, especially regarding facilities designed specifically for their use—such as schools and youth centres (Hampshire and Wilkinson, 1999). In practice, however, solutions to problems of insecurity frequently aim to exclude young people from the public domain, rather than engage them or tailor designs to their particular needs. Recent interventions include the *Mosquito* device or the playing of 'uncool' music (the so-called "Manilow method") to deter young people from 'hanging out' in public areas. Such solutions perhaps reflect a punitive approach in the UK to young people who transgress social norms of behaviour.

In the 1990s, a wider range of behaviours began to be targeted by authorities, and less serious incivilities were criminalised in the UK through the formal legal adoption of the term "antisocial" within the Crime and Disorder Act 1998. With the Act, came the Anti-social Behaviour Order (ASBO)—a civil sanction, effective for a minimum of two years. An ASBO does not result in a criminal record, but sets conditions prohibiting the offender from specific antisocial acts or entering into defined areas. While the ASBO was originally designed for use solely against adults, its popular portrayal now is as a legal measure for dealing with young people considered out-of-control. This perception is confirmed by the statistics, which show that up to the end of 2005, just over 40 per cent of ASBOs issued in England and Wales were against 10 to 17 year olds (Macdonald & Telford, 2007). In addition, a review of existing literature reveals that young people's needs are not being adequately addressed by planning and regeneration policies and practices (Day *et al*, 2011):

"Children's voices have been notably absent from UK planning and regeneration policies throughout the past two decades", and "there has been comparatively little attention to children's roles in shaping a wider regeneration agenda. It would appear there has been something of a missed opportunity..."

Day et al (2011) p. 2

4.0 ENGAGING YOUNG PEOPLE

The literature suggests that alternative, more positive, approaches to dealing with young people are desirable and possible, based on understanding, engagement and respect. In 1989, the *UN Convention of the Rights of the Child* (CRC) highlighted the need for children to participate in decision-making. This was taken forward in the UK by the 2004 Children's Act, the *Every Childs Matters* agenda and a ten-year Children Plan (DCSF, 2003, 2005). Large-scale events have been run, such as the *International Children's Conference on the Environment* and the *World Urban Forum*. Participatory design approaches, such as co-design, have also been used with young people. National programmes have attempted to improve the quality and accessibility of youth services and develop spaces tailored to the needs of young people. For example, the Netherlands' *Kids & Space* initiative involves young people in public space planning (see www.kidsandspace.nl). In Germany, *Jugend macht Stadt!* (*Youth Makes the City!*) has enabled young people to contribute to the development of cultural and physical aspects of urban environments (BMVBS, 2010a & b, www.plan-zwei.com). In addition, there are a few examples of creativity being used to engage young people in planning and design. Inter-generational 'Charrettes' use creative thinking to tackle a single issue within a specific time frame (Condon, 2008).

Participation in decision-making processes that impact on the lives of young people and on their communities is considered a fundamental right, and the basis for modern day democracy (Hart, 1992). Ideally, young people should be able to gain leverage over adults in position of power and influence, in order for ideas to be implemented and for relationships between the generations to be positively transformed. Influence over adults may emerge from the process, but results may be unexpected. For example, the *Banners for the Street* public art project in Massachusetts (USA) in the 1990s started as an arts showcase for young people, but *"... quickly took on a more political dimension when the participants discovered the poor quality of living conditions within the neighbourhood."* (Frank, 2006, p.360).

Engagement should bring benefits for young people—i.e. young people should not simply be used to serve the interests of adult stakeholders. Hart's Ladder of Children's Participation (1992) is the most widely applied scale of measurement (Day *et al*, 2011). The Ladder consists of eight rungs, the bottom three of which are classified as 'non-participation', as children's views are simply co-opted to validate adult decisions. For Hart, true participation does not begin until the fifth rung, and then escalates according to children's power to direct matters and the reducing influence exerted by adults. The top two rungs on the ladder imply a high level of independent decision-making by children, with adults performing more of the role of partners. Matthews' examination of participation in UK regeneration programmes (Matthews, 2003, p.268) focuses on the real participatory levels of Hart's ladder. Matthews identifies four different levels of engagement, ranging from 'dialogue' (listening to young people), through 'development' (adults working on behalf of and in the interests of young people), 'participation' (young people working within their communities), and 'integration' (young people working together with their communities).

It is suggested that the participation of young people in design and planning brings with it a range of benefits, including (Day et al, 2011; Frank, 2006):

- *Personal benefits to young people* – such as improved confidence, self-esteem, assertiveness and sense of control over the environment
- *Development of 'life' skills that help young people progress* – communication skills, creativity, problem solving skills, design skills, map interpretation and better understanding of community processes and the needs and perspectives of different social groups
- *Educational benefits* – related to academic achievement, attendance and behaviour at school
- *Enhanced civic and social responsibility* – including better understanding of community issues, enthusiasm for community participation, informal networking between young people, change in behaviour (toward the community and environment), increased sense of community and ownership
- *Changes to physical and social environment* – improvements in design, planning and use of space
- *Social benefits* – changes in adults' attitudes towards young people and development of better inter-generational relationships.

In relation to some projects, there is a real sense of 'distance travelled' by participants, with empirical evidence regarding the benefits to young people tending to focus on impact at the end of the intervention (Day et al, 2011). However, there is a lack of research into the longer term impact and implications of youth engagement projects. Further research also is required to more fully understand changes in perceptions of young people held by adult participants and the implications of attitudinal change for inter-generational relationships.

5.0 YOUTH DESIGN AGAINST CRIME
5.1 Background

Between 2007 and 2008, the *Design Against Crime Solution Centre* conducted a research project called *City Centre Crime: Cooling Crime Hotspots by Design*. This investigated problem areas (so-called „crime hotspots") in Manchester's city centre, and involved the development of a methodology for determining the relationship between the design, management and use of the urban environment and the crime problems occurring within it. The project resulted in 20 practical design interventions to address crime and anti-social behaviour issues (Wootton, Marselle and Davey, 2009; Wootton,

Davey and Marselle, 2011). Press coverage of the project led to the Solution Centre being contacted by UK charity Catch22 about the possibility of engaging young people in design against crime. In collaboration with Catch22 and Prudential for Youth, the Solution Centre developed the *Youth Design Against Crime* (YDAC) programme, to engage young people considered at risk of offending in generating ideas to tackle crime and anti-social behaviour problems in their neighbourhoods. YDAC draws on the Youth Action concept developed by Catch22.

5.2 The Youth Design Against Crime Programme

YDAC acknowledges that young people are too often seen only as "trouble-makers" and their opinions ignored by adults. It offers teams of young people the opportunity to challenge such stereotypes by creatively tackling crime and anti-social behaviour in their community and developing design ideas that "make a real difference". In addition, young people completing the programme and associated workbook, have the chance to gain an ASDAN Wider Skills Level 2 qualification in ‚Problem-solving' and ‚Working With Others'.

The YDAC programme is structured to run over ten to twelve weeks, as shown in Figure 1, below.

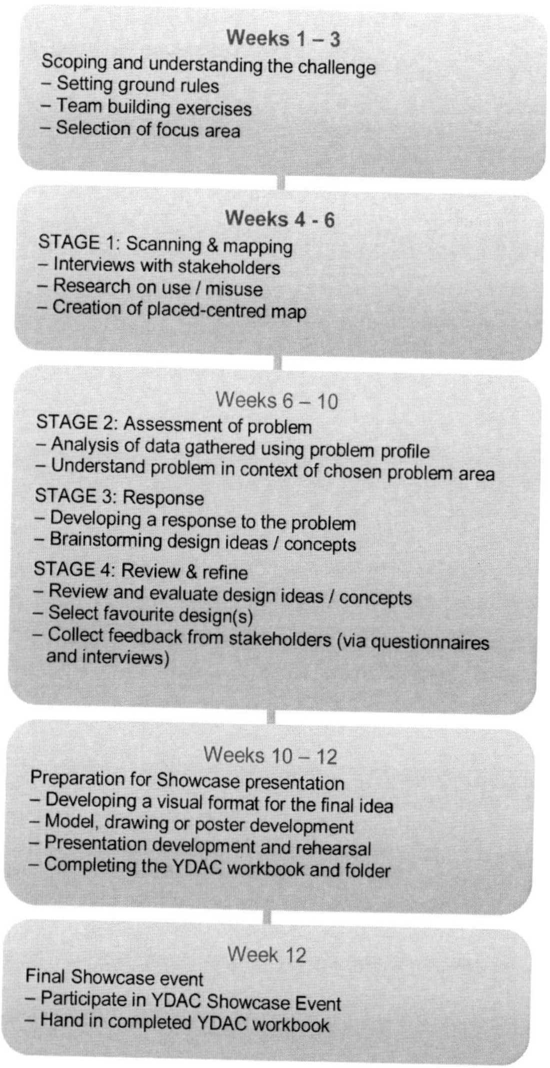

Weeks 1 – 3
Scoping and understanding the challenge
– Setting ground rules
– Team building exercises
– Selection of focus area

Weeks 4 - 6
STAGE 1: Scanning & mapping
– Interviews with stakeholders
– Research on use / misuse
– Creation of placed-centred map

Weeks 6 – 10
STAGE 2: Assessment of problem
– Analysis of data gathered using problem profile
– Understand problem in context of chosen problem area
STAGE 3: Response
– Developing a response to the problem
– Brainstorming design ideas / concepts
STAGE 4: Review & refine
– Review and evaluate design ideas / concepts
– Select favourite design(s)
– Collect feedback from stakeholders (via questionnaires and interviews)

Weeks 10 – 12
Preparation for Showcase presentation
– Developing a visual format for the final idea
– Model, drawing or poster development
– Presentation development and rehearsal
– Completing the YDAC workbook and folder

Week 12
Final Showcase event
– Participate in YDAC Showcase Event
– Hand in completed YDAC workbook

Figure 1. Example 12-week YDAC programme schedule

In the first three weeks, the young people undertake team-building activities, including identifying individual strengths and weaknesses and creating a team name. They also identify the area that will be the focus of the team's YDAC activity.

The Scanning & Mapping stage (weeks four to six) involves researching the focus area, considering why the area is important to team members, researching whether the area really has problems and understanding why. This enables young people to tackle problems of concern to them, and to use their own personal experience to identify and understand issues.

In collaboration with the police mentor, the team members must research crime and anti-social behaviour problems in the area as experienced by other users. This may involve discussions with police officers, interviews with local people (e.g. residents, shopkeepers, area management and maintenance staff) and visiting websites (e.g. www.upmystreet.com). YDAC provides the young people with a template and questions for conducting a structured interview to identify the location of problems and the causal factors associated with crime and anti-social behaviour. The research enables the young people to understand the problems and issues from the perspective of different stakeholder groups. This kicks off a process of consultation with local people, and encourages design concepts that reflect the requirements of all stakeholders.

From information collected via interviews, site visits and observation, the young people develop a 'Place-Centred Map' detailing changes in legitimate and illegitimate activity over time. For example, this might indicate where young people choose to 'hang out' (and why); and the activities taking place in different areas at different times.

Through this work, the teams identify the most common / serious crime and anti-social behaviour issues. Insight into their causes is gained by developing a 'Problem Profile'. This involves organising research findings on offenders, victims, behaviours and the environment to help identify the causal factors associated with different crime and anti-social behaviour issues. The structure and content of the Problem Profile is derived from the *Crime Lifecycle Model* developed by Wootton & Davey (2003).

In weeks six to ten, the group use creative ideation and brainstorming methods to develop design concepts in response to their research. These design ideas are evaluated by the young people in terms of their potential impact on: users; crime and anti-social behaviour; and the quality of the area. The group also considers whether any aspects of their design proposals might cause the seriousness of crime or anti-social behaviour problems to increase. A final design concept is selected and further feedback sought from stakeholders regarding its strengths and weaknesses.

In weeks ten to twelve, the young people develop drawings, models, presentation materials and argument to communicate the benefits of their final design proposal to the judging panel at the YDAC Showcase Evening. They include details of how the design was researched and developed, as well as how the team developed in terms of its thinking, skills and ability to work together.

At the showcase event, each group is given ten minutes to present their finished design in any way they choose to the judging panel and an audience of family, friends and invited stakeholders. After their presentation, the group spends five minutes answering any questions the judging panel has regarding their design idea, its implementation or the process by which it was developed. The groups are judged on: the strength of the design idea; the evidence base of the idea (including the research and consultation that was carried out); and team-working. One group is selected by the judging panel as the YDAC winner, and receives a trophy, while all runners up are awarded medals and certificates of completion.

5.3 Running YDAC projects

Five YDAC projects have been initiated to date: Greater Manchester YDAC (2009); the London borough of Southwark YDAC (2010); the London borough of Lambeth YDAC (2011); Salford YDAC (2011) and Bolton YDAC (2012). Together, these projects have directly involved over 200 young people aged between 12 and 19 years from schools and youth groups. The young people have generally poor educational backgrounds, with some having been excluded from school or involved in anti-social behaviour and identified as 'at risk of offending'.

The four teams of young people in the Greater Manchester YDAC identified the following problem areas on which to focus:

- An isolated subway (motorway underpass) close to the team's school that attracts robbery, anti-social behaviour and serious crime.
- A pedestrian route to a local shopping precinct with several problems. For example, groups of street drinkers congregating on the public seating, creating a climate of fear.
- A local public park and sports ground that is underused (except by drug dealers and their clients), poorly lit, poorly maintained and considered unsafe by local residents.
- The playing field next to the team's youth centre, which has become a hot spot for drug dealing.

At the final showcase event in November 2009, all four teams presented their design interventions. A Judging Panel made up of senior decision-makers working in the areas of crime and community safety in Greater Manchester were tasked with selecting the winning team. Inspired by the high standard of the ideas, the judges pledged on the night to provide funding to implement the design solutions of all four teams.

Figure 2. A team presents their ideas at the London Borough of Southwark YDAC Showcase Evening

The YDAC projects delivered in London and Bolton differ slightly from the original 2009 Greater Manchester programme, as these each involved groups of young people from a single school—so-called 'alternative curriculum' students. This meant that their YDAC activities were undertaken as part of their school lessons, falling under the subject area of 'citizenship'.

Figure 4. One of the teams with their Police Mentor at the YDAC Showcase Evening

Figure 5. Young people and judges at the London Borough of Southwark YDAC Showcase Evening

The YDAC teams impressed the judges with the quality of their proposed solutions and the creativity of their ideas. A Lambeth YDAC team called 'Kick Out Crime" (from Lilian Baylis Technology School) perceived a problem with anti-social behaviour in a local park. However, consultation revealed the main problem to be dog fouling. The team proposed a dedicated area for dogs, funded by dog owners—'dog paradise'. Fines for dog fouling was also proposed (i.e. a criminal record for dogs). Solutions were also innovative. A YDAC team from Greater Manchester tacked the problem of public seating on a pedestrian route to a local shopping precinct being used by drinkers and generating fear. Police had considered asking the local authority to remove the seating, but removal would be a problem for legitimate users. The young people suggested that individuals seats spaced apart.

At the showcase events, the judges committed to implementing ideas generated by the teams of young people. This clearly made the young people extremely proud. However, the Solution Centre and Catch22 wanted more detailed information about changes in attitudes and perceptions amongst the young people. An evaluation of the first four YDAC projects was undertaken by the Design Against Crime Solution Centre with funding from Catch22 and the University of Salford.

5.4 Evaluating YDAC

The evaluation aimed to identify the impact of YDAC on young people and adult participants, and provide recommendations on how the design and delivery of the YDAC programme might be improved. Focus groups were conducted with young people, youth workers and police mentors, and telephone interviews with Showcase Evening judges.

Findings show that young people had doubts and reservations about the YDAC programme, when it was first presented at the Launch Event. YDAC was perceived as just another school project that would yield little benefit for young people. Some young people exhibited low levels of self-esteem, assuming that their involvement in YDAC was because they were *"bad"*. Others doubted their ability to complete the programme.

"I just didn't think that we would have got a good enough idea to make it all the way to the end, to the final."

Young person

YDAC presented a number of challenges for the young people to overcome. Some had to get to know team members, and participants reported feeling *"shy"* when first confronted with new social situations. Some individuals were unwilling to contribute to the work of the team, which presented difficulties for other team members. Young people had to cope with the stress of identifying and developing a suitable design solution to present at the final event. They also had to complete the YDAC Workbook, which was considered relatively academic by youth workers and not something the young people would normally do.

Over the course of YDAC, the young people developed a strong team spirit. As they became aware of strengths and weaknesses within their team, they demonstrated their ability to help those individuals who had problems. This team spirit was evident from the shared sense of pride felt by participants on completing the YDAC project.

Interviewer:	*Even if you didn't win, did you still feel proud of each other? That you'd done it?*
All:	*Yeah.*
Young Person 1:	*We'd done it to the end, so we started and we finished.*
Young Person 2:	*In our heads, we won anyway.*
Young Person 3:	*No. We actually won for completing a whole project.*
Young Person 2:	*Did we?*
Young Person 3:	*Yeah. We was winners. We all done the whole project.*
Young Person 4:	*Saw it through to the end.*
All:	*Yeah!*

Focus Group

Focus group findings confirmed that the young people were the prime decision-makers in terms of both the problems upon which to focus, and the design ideas to develop and present at the Showcase Evening.

"The thing I liked about it: we chose where we can work; what place we can work on. They [youth workers and police mentors] never chose for us."

Young person

Youth workers stated that being given responsibility for decision-making motivated the group:

"They [the young people] actually took full ownership of it... They were as excited, or more excited than the staff in the end."

Youth worker

Participation in the YDAC project improved the confidence, knowledge and skills of the young people.

"I like the fact that people were confident enough to speak up and talk to an audience."

Young Person

Participant from three focus groups said they had developed research skills through taking part in the YDAC programme:

"Getting research, and then seeing it in different aspects... Like how you could change it—the problems there, like. And speaking to other people and hearing different comments, and then making one final view of their state."

Young person

Young people were able to overcome fears about talking in public and deal with setbacks. They were also able to use their confidence and skills positively by, for example, talking to the community, presenting their ideas on stage and generating ideas to address problems. Young people often have direct experience of crime and anti-social behaviour and therefore bring new insights to design activities. For one participant, this development in confidence was described as *"life-changing"*.

Young person:	*It was life changing...*
Interviewer:	*How did it change your life?*
Young person:	*I wasn't confident.*

Focus Group

When interviewed, young people said how 'proud' they felt—for winning, for coming second or for completing the programme. Participants were aware that they had seen something through to the end—which is typically difficult for this group of young people.

"I was proud of my group... I loved them. 'Cos we won and we done great!"

Young person

"I was proud because we came second!"

Young person

"Everyone took part and said: if we win or we lose we're still, like, still going to do it. So everyone was proud of each other really."

Young person

The sense of achievement felt by young people was clearly evident to those watching the Showcase event. An intentional 'side effect' of the YDAC process is that it helped generate better relationships between the young people and teachers, residents, community workers and the police. As one police mentor remarked:

"... I feel I have broken down a barrier between myself as a Police Officer and the group. What I have been a part of in the past few weeks has opened my eyes and made me realise that these young people really do care about their community and really do want to make a big difference."

Police Mentor

Another police officer stated that she is now able to chat to members of her team when she sees them in the neighbourhood. A schoolteacher said that her relationship to class members has improved, since completing YDAC.

While judges may pledge funding for good ideas, funding or feedback about progress is not always forthcoming. Some focus groups members felt that this was demotivating for young people.

6.0 DISCUSSION & CONCLUSION

YDAC demonstrates that young people at risk of offending can successfully design against crime. However, the ability to engage this group of young people and support them in their efforts to develop solutions to local problems depends on the design and delivery of the programme.

6.1 Personal development

Young people participating in YDAC must be given the opportunity to learn about research, design and the communication of ideas. Indeed, really understanding problems and needs is the key to developing successful new designs. The authors believe that the research process is central to the success of YDAC and that the 'creative challenge' nature of YDAC is an important component. In the authors' opinion, providing a more simplified, less-challenging process (for example, by reducing the need for the teams to understand the problem, its context, or others' perspectives) would significantly reduce the personal impact experienced by the young people—as well as leading to less valuable design solutions being developed and potentially implemented.

To be able to develop the necessary skills and address the challenges, young people must be supported by motivated youth workers, police mentors and teachers. Youth workers had an important role to play in helping young people overcome lack of confidence and motivation, as well as in dealing with specific personal issues that arose. On rare occasions where a police mentor or teacher was not fully engaged in YDAC, it proved difficult for young people to develop innovative design ideas and for better relationships between young people and adult participants to be generated.

6.2 Tackling real issues

Young people address real issues of concern to them and their community. Being given responsibility for tackling real world issues helps generate in the young people a sense of ownership of the project and intrinsic motivation to create a good design. In addition, young people—especially those at risk of offending—bring to their projects a level of 'inside knowledge' and insight into the issues in their local areas that is often simply unavailable to outsiders. For example, one group of young people identified problems related to prostitution in their area about which the police had no prior knowledge. This opportunity to use their insight into the issues in a constructive way is empowering for young people and potentially enables them to gain some leverage over adults in positions of power.

Responsibility for decisions on choice of focus areas and creative design solutions rests with the young people participating in a YDAC project. They identify the problem area on which their team will focus, and select the design ideas that will be developed and presented at the Showcase Evening. The evaluation confirmed that youth workers and police mentors act as advisors, supporting the work of the team and enabling specific actions, such as liaison with local residents and businesses, or providing more detail on crime problems. The evaluation of YDAC reinforces literature on the importance of young people's ability to make decisions about issues that impact on their lives and to benefit from the process (Hart,1992)

6.3 Benefits for young people
The YDAC programme offers significant benefits to young people. Participation in YDAC increases the young people's sense of accomplishment and self-confidence, raising self-esteem through involvement in activities of benefit to the community, rather than through rebellious or aggressive behaviour (Lo *et al*, 2011). Presenting at the Showcase Evening is both daunting and exciting, and generates a real sense of team spirit and accomplishment for the participants. There is a real sense of 'distance travelled' for YDAC participants (Day *et al*, 2011, p. 62). Changes in behaviour and attitudes are all the more significant due to YDAC's targeting of young people considered "at risk" by police and school authorities.

6.4 Transforming intergenerational relationships
YDAC brought about changes in attitudes amongst adult participants. Most significantly, YDAC built bridges between young people and police mentors and teachers. The Showcase Event also changed attitudes towards young people amongst members of the judging panel. The YDAC process requires young people to understand the behaviour of all the users of an area—both legitimate users and offenders—in order to generate solutions. This means consulting with different stakeholders and attempting to understand issues from their perspectives. This has the practical benefit of helping the teams come up with better design ideas. Importantly, it also has a 'community building' effect, helping build bridges between the young people and different social groups in their neighbourhood.

The evaluation showed that further steps must be taken to support improved relationships with the wider community. In the most recent Bolton YDAC, delivered after the evaluation, budget was allocated to providing free coaches to bring family and community members to the Showcase Evening venue. In the future, resources would ideally be dedicated to communicating young people's work and achievements to the wider community.

6.5 Young people and urban regeneration

The teams of young people present the design solutions they have researched and developed to a panel of judges. Judges are often members of UK Community Safety Partnerships (previously called Crime & Disorder Reduction Partnerships). However, the YDAC programme was not designed as a consultation method for use in urban planning projects or regeneration programmes, but to meet the needs of the participating young people. While YDAC does not claim to generate solutions to problems on behalf of other stakeholder groups, the organisers nevertheless take steps to maximise the potential for ideas to be taken forward. In particular, efforts are made to select judges with responsibility for community safety, regeneration, urban planning and development. As a result of being members of Community Safety Partnerships, judges may be able to allocate resources to implementation. This increases the possibility that positive comments by judges on an idea's quality will be followed up with action on its implementation.

Promises have been made to implement ideas presented by at least one team of young people at all Showcase Evenings held between 2009 and 2012. YDAC organisers emphasise that there is no guarantee *any* of the young people's ideas will be implemented. But promises made on the night of the Showcase event inevitably raises expectations amongst participants. The organisers are aware that promises may not come to fruition, and that even if they do, the process of implementation can lengthy. A YDAC team's designs for improving a problematic underpass, for example, took two years to become a reality. To address this issue, effort needs to be directed at managing expectations amongst participants, both at the YDAC Launch Event and following the Showcase Evening. Ideally, resources need to be dedicated to monitoring and supporting the uptake of ideas generated and communicating progress to young people and adult participants.

The value of engaging young people in planning, development and regeneration procedures is emphasised in the literature (Matthews, 2003; Frank, 2006). Although supportive of efforts to consult, the authors are aware of practical difficulties of incorporating young people into planning processes. The activities undertaken by young people would have to suit the objectives and schedule of development and planning processes—which often have long timeframes and are slow to make progress. The authors believe that the process of engagement and involvement of young people should be tailored to the needs and interests of the particular target group.

6.6 Reducing crime and anti social behaviour

Solutions developed by young people are sometimes implemented and thus help to reduce problems of crime and antisocial behaviour. In addition, the skills gained through YDAC may help divert young people away from offending and anti-social behaviour by building self-esteem, fostering teamwork and enabling young people to collaborate in achieving a goal of benefit to the community. YDAC may also act as a catalyst for teachers and parents, showing young people in a new light. Through better publicity and follow-up of YDAC ideas generated, the community can be made more aware of the young people's commitment to their neighbourhood. Research shows that offenders are prone to negative beliefs and emotions, focus on short-term life goals and may adopt a confrontational style (Burt *et al*, 2006). Acting rebelliously and aggressively in front of peers may also be a misguided means of boosting self-esteem (Hales, 2006; Lo *et al*, 2011). The advantage of YDAC is that it encourages peers to work together in pursuit of a shared civic goal.

There is a risk, however, that positive changes in attitudes and relationships engendered by YDAC will not be sustained. Ideally, programme organisers would have access to other processes (such as mentors) for supporting ongoing development of young people from deprived backgrounds. They would also explore whether families of young people could be more engaged in the programme.

6.7 Rolling out YDAC

In partnership with Catch22 and partners in several EU states, the Design Against Crime Solution Centre is exploring ways in which YDAC might be rolled out as a national programme in the UK, and how it might be piloted in other European contexts. In the UK, the target group has been young people at risk of offending. Two models have been piloted to deliver YDAC to this target group: (i) Alternative curriculum groups in schools; and (ii) Youth or community groups. In Europe, or internationally, the target group may be young people interested in participating in democratic processes related to government or urban development—rather than those at risk of offending. There may be little or no intention to divert young people away from offending. The delivery model might be also be different. While YDAC could certainly be adapted to different contexts, we believe that the programme should continue to prioritise meeting the needs of young people. The engagement of 'hard to reach' young people requires that programmes are carefully designed and effectively delivered by professionals skilled at working with young people. In this respect, the authors acknowledge the role of Norman Lloyd from Catch22, who has years of experience of inspiring and supporting young people from deprived backgrounds.

ACKNOWLEDGEMENTS

The authors would like to thank:

- Catch22, especially Norman Lloyd, who initiated the development of the YDAC programme and manages its delivery. HEFCE UnLtd, Prudential for Youth and J.P. Morgan for funding the delivery of YDAC
- Bethany Higson, University of Salford, who conducted the focus groups and interviews for the evaluation of YDAC. The evaluation was funded by Catch22 and the University of Salford.
- Paul van Soomeren and Sander Flight, DSP-groep (Netherlands) and Dr Klaus Habermann-Niesse, Plan Zwei (Germany) for information about youth, design and planning programmes in Europe.

7.0 REFERENCES

BMVBS (2010a) *"Jungend Macht Stadt"*, Bundesministerium fuer Verkehr, Bau und Stadtentwicklung, Berlin: Germany. Available for download from http://www.bmvbs.de/cae/servlet/ contentblob/59406/publicationFile/30662/jugend-macht-stadt-publikation.pdf

BMVBS (2010b) *"Freiraeume Fuer Kinder and Jugendliche"*, Praxis Heft 70. Bundesministerium fuer Verkehr, Bau und Stadtentwicklung, Berlin: Germany. Available from silvia.wicharz@bbr.bund.de.

Burt, Callie Harbin, Simons Ronald L, and Simons, Leslie, G. (2006) "A Longitudinal Test of the Effects of Parenting and the Stability of Self-control: Negative Evidence for the General Theory of Crime". *Criminology*, Vol. 44: No. 2, pp. 353–396.

Condon, P.M (2008) "Design Charrrettes for Sustainable Communities", Island Press: Washington, United States.

Davey, C.L., and Wootton, A.B. (forthcoming) *"Crime and the Urban Environment: The Implications for Wellbeing"*, in *"Wellbeing. A Complete Reference Guide"* (Eds) Burton, R., Davies-Cooper,R. and Cooper, C. Wiley-Blackwell: Chichester (UK).

Davey, C.L., Wootton, A.B. and Marselle, M. (2012) Engaging Young People in Design Against Crime. Design Research. *Swedish Design Research Journal*, 1, 12, 29 – 38

Davey, C.L., Wootton, A.B., Thomas, A., Cooper, R. and Press, M. (2005) "Design for the Surreal World?: A New Model of Socially Responsible Design." *Refereed conference proceedings for the European Academy of Design*, 29th to 31st March, Bremen, Germany. ISBN 3899572907

Davey, C.L., Cooper, R. and Press, M. (2002) *Design Against Crime: Case Study Exemplars*. Design Policy Partnership, University of Salford.

Day, L., Sutton, L. and Jenkins, S. (2011) *"Children and Young People's Participation in Planning and Regeneration"*. A Final Report to the Ecorys Research Programme 2010-11. Ecorys: Birmingham, UK. Available from http://www.uk.ecorys.com/news/april2011/children-young-people-report.html

DCSF (2003) *"Every Child Matters"* [online]. London, UK: HMSO. Available from: http://www.education.gov.uk/consultations/downloadableDocs/EveryChildMatters.pdf [Accessed 12.09.11]

DCSF (2005) *"Youth Matters"* [online]. London, UK: HMSO. Available from: http://www.napta.org.uk/resources/youth_matters.pdf [Accessed 12.09.11]

Design Council (2011) *Designing Out Crime. A Designer's guide*. Design Council: London, UK. Original research conducted by Design Against Crime Solution Centre, University of Salford. Available for download from: http://www.designcouncil.org.uk/Documents/Documents/OurWork/Crime/designersGuide_digital.pdf

Design Council (2003) *Think Thief: A Designer's Guide to Designing Out Crime*. Design Council and Design Policy Partnership. Design Council: London, UK

Fionda, J. (2005) "Devils and Angels. Youth Policy and Crime. Hart Publishing: Portland, USA.

Flatley, J. Kershaw, C., Smith, K, Chaplin R. and Moon, D. (2010) "Crime in England and Wales 2009/10. Findings from the British Crime Survey and police recorded crime" (Second Edition). *Home Office Statistical Bulletin*. 12/10, July 2010. http://rds.homeoffice.gov.uk/rds/pdfs10/hosb1210.pdf

Farrington, D.P. (1986) "Age and crime" in Tonry, M. and Morris, N. (Eds) *Crime and Justice: An annual review of research* Vol 7, pp. 189–250

Frank, K.I. (2006) The Potential of Youth Participation in Planning. *Journal of Planning Literature*, Vol. 20, No. 4, pp. 351–371.

Hales, J., Nevill, C., Pudney, S. and Tipping, S. (2009) Longitudinal Analysis of the Offending, Crime and Justices Survey, 2003-06. Key Implications. Research Report 19, Home Office, November 2009.ISBN 978-1-84987-100-6. Available for download from:

http://webarchive.nationalarchives.gov.uk/20110218135832/rds.homeoffice.gov.uk/rds/pdfs09/horr19c.pdf

Hart, R.A (1992) *Children's participation: From tokenism to Citizenship*. Unicef: Florence, Italy

Hampshire, R. and Wilkinson, M. (1999) *Youth Shelters and Sports Systems*. Thames Valley Police. London.

Lo, T.W, Cheng, C.H.K., Wong, D.S.W. and Rochelle, T.L, and Kwok, S.I. (2011) Self-Esteem, Self-efficacy and Deviant Behaviour of Young People in Hong Kong. *Advances in Applied Sociology*, Vol. 1, No. 1, 48-55.

Macdonald, S and Telford, M (2007) The use of ASBOs against young people in England and Wales: lessons from Scotland. *Legal Studies*, Vol. 27 No. 4, December 2007, pp. 604–629.

McVie, S. (2005) Patterns of Deviance underlying the Age-crime Curve: The Long Term Evidence. *British Society of Criminology E-Journal*, Vol. 7, 1–15. http://www.britsoccrim.org/volume7/007.pdf

Matthews, H. (2003) Children and Regeneration: Setting an Agenda for Community Participation and Integration. *Children and Society*, 17(4), pp.264-276.

Roe,S. and Ashe, J. (2008) „Young people and crime: findings from the 2006 Offending, Crime and Justice Survey". Home Office Statistical Bulletin, 09/08, 15 July 2008. http://rds.homeoffice.gov.uk/rds/pdfs08/hosb0908.pdf

Van Dijk, J., van Kesteren, J. and Smit, P. (2007) Criminal Victimisation in International Perspective. key findings from the 2004 – 2005 ICVS and EU ICS. WODC: Den Haag, Netherlands.

Waiton, S. (2006) "Anti-social behaviour: the construction of a crime". *Spiked*. Thursday 19th January.

Wootton, A.B. & Davey, C.L. (2012) "Embedding Crime Prevention within Design", in Ekblom, P. (Guest Ed), "Design Against Crime. Crime Proofing Everyday Products". Crime Prevention Series, Vol. 27, Ronald.V. Clarke, (Series Editor).

Wootton, A.B., Davey, C.L. and Marselle, M. (2011) *Design Against Crime: A Catalyst for Change Amongst Young People*, 9th European Academy of Design conference "The Endless End", Porto, Portugal, 4–7 May 2011. http://endlessend.up.pt/site/wp-content/uploads/2011/05/EAD9-Conference-Proceedings_r.pdf

Wootton, A.B., Marselle, M. and Davey, C.L. (2009) *City Centre Crime: Design Thinking for Safer City Centres*. 8th European Academy of Design Conference, The Robert Gordon University, Aberdeen, Scotland, 1–3 April 2009. http://usir.salford.ac.uk/12531/

Wootton, A.B. and Davey, C.L. (2005) *Design Against Crime Evaluation Framework. A Framework to Support & Evaluate the Integration of Design Against Crime within Development Projects*. Design Against Crime Solution Centre: Salford.

Wootton, A. B. and Davey, C.L. (2003) *Crime Lifecycle: Guidance for Generating Design Against Crime Ideas*. The University of Salford: Salford. (Translated into German in 2007).

Please address correspondence to:

Dr Caroline L. Davey
Director

Design Against Crime Solution Centre
University of Salford
Centenary Building
Peru Street
Salford M3 6EQ
United Kingdom

E: c.davey@salford.ac.uk

International Centre for the Prevention of Crime (ICPC)

2012 International Report on Crime Prevention and Community Safety

Executive Summary

The International Centre for the Prevention of Crime's 2012 *International Report on Crime Prevention and Community Safety* analyzes current and relevant topics in crime, to develop ways in which crime prevention can contribute to social cohesion and resilient communities.

Produced every two years, this third edition of the Report focuses on five topics of significance for crime prevention policymaking at the international level: Human Trafficking, Informal Settlements, Post-Conflict and Post-Disaster Areas, Drug Production in Developed Countries and ICPC's own Global Survey on Safety in Cities. The Report is also enriched by a number of Special Contributions from experts and practitioners, who bring their particular view of the issues raised in the Report, as well as Case Studies that provide original research on ongoing challenges and existing international prevention practices.

The *International Report* provides information and tools to help governments, local authorities, international organizations and other actors implement successful crime prevention policies in their countries or cities. Thus the *International Report on Crime Prevention and Community Safety* asserts itself as a crucial tool in the design and implementation of safety and prevention policies.

Introduction and Crime Overview

A Rights-Based Approach to Crime Prevention: Overview of ICPC's work

Crime prevention and community safety entail a wide variety of principles that aim to promote the values of equality, education, freedom from persecution, and many other rights to which individuals as well as communities are entitled. **Chapter One** presents the framework and principles in which ICPC places crime prevention as well as key concepts used throughout the Report. It defines crime prevention in a broad sense as including developmental, social, situational and recidivism prevention. It outlines the key notions as well as the conceptual basis of the UN's Guidelines for the Prevention of Crime, all of which form the essence of ICPC's work. Thus ICPC understands crime prevention as a series of actions that (UNODC/ICPC 2011):

1. *Promote the well-being of people and encourage positive behaviour through social, economic, health and educational measures, with a particular emphasis on children youth and women, and focus on the risk and protective factors associated with crime and victimization.*

2. *Change the conditions in neighbourhoods that influence offending, victimization, and the insecurity that results from crime by building on the initiatives, expertise and commitment of community members.*

3. *Prevent the occurrences of crime by reducing opportunities, increasing risk of being apprehended and minimizing benefits, including through environmental design, and by providing assistance and information to potential and actual victims.*

4. *Prevent recidivism by assisting the social reintegration of offenders and other preventive mechanisms.*

5. *Include a wide range of actors such as police forces, courts and civil society in the development of crime prevention policy.*

Crime Overview and Trends to Watch: Challenges for Crime Prevention

Crime rates and perceptions of insecurity fluctuate constantly. In an ever more connected world, the behaviour of crime and policy in one region of the world can have worldwide effects. Policymakers are more pressed than ever to deal with issues of local and transnational crime by their constituents as new challenges emerge to contest current policy. **Chapter Two** explores current debates on crime as a way to contextualize the analytical parts of the *2012 International Report*. It addresses the puzzling decrease in crime rates that the developed world (especially the US) has seen in the last 20 years and finds that there is an ongoing debate in the literature as to the factors that determine this decrease, such as better policing, immigration, social development in urban areas and higher rates of incarceration. On this last factor the *2012 International Report* explores the debate on whether higher incarceration rates actually contribute to the decrease of crime rates. Current research agrees that, while high incarceration rates are correlated to drops in crime, it is not clear whether they have actually caused it. Indeed, available evidence suggests that initially an increase in prison sentences may result in lower crime rates but this ceases to be so after incarceration continues to increase, suggesting that it has a short lived effect. It is also clear that decreases in crime rates will still occur regardless of correctional policy and due to other factors such as better policing and social development.

A good measure of crime rates is the homicide rate and the available literature on it suggests that globally trends in homicide are varied. While Western Europe, North America (the US and Canada) and Oceania have seen varying degrees of decreases in their homicide rates, Central America and Sub-Saharan Africa have seen significant increases in their rates. Central America is a region that has been especially affected by this escalation. This change is accounted for by shifts in the drug trade and its flows, the growing presence of drug trafficking gangs, regional structural disadvantages and overtly coercive government responses. These scenarios present a challenge for crime prevention which is underlined by the need to produce better and diverse data on crime to better inform policy responses. In addition, Chapter Two highlights two trends to watch in the near future, namely counterfeit medications – an illicit activity that kills close to 700,000 people in Africa alone yearly - and crime in public transport, where innovations in crime prevention from Mexico City to Japan are proving that they can contribute to a better living experience for dwellers of mega-cities.

Crime Prevention in Different and Challenging Settings

The 2012 edition of the *International Report* underscores the importance and impact of crime prevention in a variety of challenging settings that impact the lives of millions of people worldwide, using actual contexts (Post-Conflict and Post-Disaster areas and Informal Settlements) and illicit activities (human trafficking and drug production).

Human Trafficking and Exploitation: The New Faces of Slavery from a Prevention Perspective

Human Trafficking and exploitation are crimes that affect millions of people all over the world. In this context, it has become a priority on the agenda of many governments and organizations. **Chapter Three** tracks the evolution of the phenomena by researching national laws and national action plans in human trafficking for all countries in the world. The research has shown important results. National level laws are common. Out of 193 countries, 140 were found to have some form of national legislation that addresses this issue. Chapter Three also identifies National Action plans in at least 80 countries. Those countries that have developed national action plans do tend to include in them various levels of prevention, mostly in the form of social/community based programmes as well as developmental programmes. The links between human trafficking and exploitation (in cases such as slavery, debt bondage or labour exploitation) are highlighted throughout the chapter as two faces of the same coin. This chapter is illustrated by two national case studies, Ukraine and Peru, two countries that have made substantial advances in preventing human trafficking within their national policies.

Informal Settlements: Spaces full of possibilities for Community safety approaches

Over a billion people live in informal settlements and slums in the world. While these communities have enormous potential, crime and violence have frequently hampered their development and their acquisition of full citizenship rights. **Chapter Four** explores the hugely diverse of ways in which these communities have worked to prevent crime and violence. High crime rates in these settlements are often determined by unemployment, discrimination, lack of access to rights and family related problems such as substance abuse. Issues of disenfranchisement are common and many of the inhabitants of these areas have low access to citizenship rights and social services common to the rest of the population. There exist many potential strategies for tackling crime in informal settlements. Examples from Chapter Four highlight the absolute need for a number of factors to be present in order to create successful local programmes: 1) programmes must be inclusive of all actors; unilateral decisions and strategies are not always conducive to successful scenarios, 2) a long-term view and commitment from all actors that moves beyond political time-frames is an important tool for the implementation of programmes that effectively strengthen the community 3) the provision of rights such as health and education as well as land rights can be concurrent with local, mid-term solutions such as urban upgrading and community building exercises and both spectrums contribute to peaceful and resilient communities. The presence of these factors can result in better and more successful policies. Case studies include South Africa and Brazil and focus on two innovative urban safety programmes in those countries.

Post-conflict and Post-disaster areas: Crime Prevention as a positive way to create a peaceful environment

Post-conflict and Post-disaster areas present some of the most challenging contexts in terms of safety and security. In the aftermath of a conflict, establishing a minimum of security is paramount for the success of Disarmament, Demobilisation and Reintegration (DDR) processes. Crime and violence has been shown in many cases to increase in the period following a natural disaster such as an earthquake or a flood. **Chapter Five** explores the potential for crime prevention in these sensitive contexts. Crime prevention and community safety are not concepts easily found in post-conflict and post-disaster interventions today. While recognising the immense difficulties that first responders, governments, international organisations and other actors face in the process of DDR and post-conflict state building or in responding to a natural disaster, there is indeed a place and need for crime prevention in these contexts. Based on the notion that safety is one of the first goals and a precondition to peace and development, Chapter Five shows how crime prevention can offer strategies by which communities may achieve higher levels of safety both at the onset of the intervention and as a long term strategy in physical reconstruction or post-conflict state building. The cases of Haiti and Mozambique are used to illustrate the potential and challenges for crime prevention in these contexts.

Drug Production in Developed Countries: Challenges to local safety

Developed countries have been emerging as leading producers and exporters of certain illicit drugs worldwide, namely cannabis and synthetic drugs such as ecstasy and amphetamines.

Chapter Six addresses the number of possible negative consequences of this trend on community safety. First, the presence of drugs in a community (whether for production or consumption) can have a negative impact on the population. This may manifest itself as crime related to the production of drugs such as the presence of gangs, as well as health factors derived from local consumption. Secondly, this activity opens the door to the insertion into the community of larger organized crime groups seeking to profit from the drug market. Thus, identifying at-risk populations and implementing preventive early interventions to avoid the insertion of drug production into a community can have positive effects.

Furthermore prevention is helpful in finding pertinent strategies for communities already affected by this illegal activity to tackle victimisation. On the other hand there are high costs in the public health arena associated with the presence of drugs in a community. Drug production may be local, serving only local markets when production is low. However as production increases and surplus production is achieved, it may become part of transnational networks of drug trafficking, extending its impact beyond the local community. The transnational drug trade fuels large networks of illegal activity in production, transit and consumer countries and is also connected to other types of crime such as human trafficking, extortion and corruption. Chapter Six explores how all of this can seriously harm social cohesion within communities and lead to low levels of trust, high crime rates and a decline in the quality of life of the community. Canada is explored as the case study in this chapter, highlighting local issues as well as programmes used to tackle the problem of internal drug markets.

Safety in Cities: ICPC's 2011 Global Survey

Urban safety is a central subject to cities around the world. Precise and useful information is needed to respond to the safety needs of communities and policymakers all over the world. In an attempt to gather information on the role and action of local authorities in crime prevention and community safety in a systematic manner, **Chapter Seven** presents the results of the very first Global Survey on Safety in Cities, an ICPC initiative to generate solid and detailed information on actual local prevention programmes worldwide. This chapter analyses issues such as the prevalence of crime prevention programmes at the city level, the budgets for these programmes, whether or not these are evaluated, and who finances them, as well as giving specific details about the programmes themselves, such as which types of crimes they tackle. Information is also included about important issues in cities such as drugs, gangs and armed violence. The Survey is a significant step within long-standing efforts to support crime prevention with solid and reliable data. Overall, this chapter offers a detailed glimpse of the possibilities and potential of a worldwide crime prevention database.

Key Messages of the International Report

- Safety should be understood as a right to which communities and citizens are entitled. As such, it provides a framework of action for governments and any actors involved in procuring this vital public good.

- An understanding of safety as a public good, cooperation and partnership between actors (public, private and civil society) is more important than ever in order to sustain healthy communities, especially in times of financial uncertainty.

- Although not always a priority in contexts of conflict and natural disasters, safety and crime prevention are vital ingredients for successful interventions and hold enormous potential when properly implemented in these areas, helping tackle feelings of insecurity exacerbated by the crisis as well as generating long-term safer communities.

- Processes of urbanization have resulted in a majority of people living in cities today; in this context, urban crime can affect large numbers of people and has become one of the most important challenges for policymakers at all levels, especially for city governments.

- Improving living standards in informal urban settlements, coupled with overall efforts in crime prevention can contribute significantly to making cities more secure but this effect is only achievable when implemented as part of a global strategy.

- The design and implementation of National Action Plans that include prevention as a key ingredient is a positive step forward in preventing and combatting human trafficking and exploitation.

- Investment at the community level can contribute to building resilient communities, where crime prevention interventions have a greater chance of success when it comes to avoiding the presence and settlement of drug producers and traffickers.

- Developed countries need to include prevention strategies in their drug policies as a way to address the growing issue of internal drug production, especially of cannabis and methamphetamines and other related synthetic drugs such as MDMA, and as a way of tackling demand for narcotics.

- Crime and the fear of crime appear to be an important concern even in settings and countries where crime rates have decreased. In this context, although crime prevention is increasing its presence in the safety agenda of many countries, it is still not a central policy ingredient alongside criminal justice policies and programmes.

- There is a general lack of evaluation of safety and security programmes that needs to be addressed in the near future. Evidence should be at the centre of any policymaking process and cost benefit analyses can contribute to advance the crime prevention agenda.

For further information, please contact us at:
International Centre for the Prevention of Crime
465, rue St-Jean, suite 803, Montreal, (Quebec)
H2Y 2R6, CANADA
Email: cipc@crime-prevention-intl.org

The *2012 International Report on Crime Prevention and Community Safety* will be available in May in English, French and Spanish on the ICPC Website www.crime-prevention-intl.org

Tina Silbernagl / Philipp Kuehl

Systemic approaches and collaborative action for realizing community safety- experiences from South Africa

"In 2030, people living in South Africa feel safe at home, at school and at work, and they enjoy a community life free of fear. Women walk freely in the streets and children play safely outside. The police service is well-resourced and professional, staffed by highly skilled officers who value their work, serve the community, safeguard lives and property without discrimination, protect the peaceful against violence, and respect the rights of all to equality and justice."[1]

This is the ambitious vision for safer communities in South Africa in 2030, as laid out in the country's recently released National Development Plan. The plan "recognizes that achieving long-term, sustainable safety requires an integrated approach focused on tackling the fundamental causes of criminality. This requires mobilizing a wider range of state and non-state capacities and resources at all levels and active citizen's involvement and co-responsibility."[2]

This article looks at some of the challenges and opportunities regarding integrated approaches to community safety in South Africa and provides snapshots of three existing initiatives[3] that attempt to give expression to the more systemic, multi-stakeholder and collaborative approaches called for in the National Development Plan. These examples were presented by a South African delegation to the German Congress on Crime Prevention Annual International Forum in Munich in April 2012, which formed part of a study tour led by the Deutsche Gesellschaft für Internationale Zusammenarbeit (GIZ). Although they are not intended to present a collective approach the case studies give a glimpse into what is being done at different levels. The article also offers some perspectives on the potential for the concept of integrated approaches and demands that such promising practices are more widely disseminated and replicated, which is one of the primary goals of the Inclusive Violence Prevention Programme implemented by GIZ on behalf of the Federal Ministry for Economic Cooperation and Development.

---

[1] National Planning Commission South Africa: National Development Plan: Vision for 2030. (P. 349 – 363). 2011.
[2] See above
[3] Contributions by: Dr. Barbara Holtmann, Consultant and Researcher
    Nazira Cachali, Programme Manager "Jo'burg City Safety Programme"
    Dr. Gilbert Lawrence, Head of Western Cape Department of Community Safety

Understanding violence

The drivers of crime and violence are varied and complex, and are invariably intricately connected to specific local circumstances. However, there are a number of trends that are globally conducive to crime and violence. One is the rapid pace of urbanization, which presents huge challenges for the populations living in many urban areas. For the first time ever, more than half of the world's population lives in towns and cities. In South Africa, more than half of the population currently lives and works in urban areas, which are continuing to grow. With this dramatic shift come enormous problems of social inequality, unemployment and urban poverty that are most visible in communities lacking access to basic services such as health, quality education, housing or decent work. Many of South Africa's urban areas are insufficiently equipped to cope with rapid urbanization, especially the large township areas, a problematic legacy of Apartheid planning, that typically lack adequate infrastructure and services. In many cases high levels of discontent and anger with lacking basic services are the results, which in turn increase the likelihood of crime and violent behaviour.

However, given that the phenomenon of violence is a more complex issue that results from the interplay of a multitude of different factors, there is no single reason that sufficiently explains why some individuals behave violently towards others or why violence is more prevalent in some communities than in others. The ecological model developed by the World Health Organisation (WHO) offers a very useful description of the multifaceted nature of violence. WHO differentiates between risk factors occurring at the individual, relationship, community and societal levels, which influence young people[4] in particular and affect their vulnerability to violent behaviour:

---

[4] Drawing on the global wealth of experience and academic insights, GIZ developed a practice-oriented model which is intended to assist in the planning of complex crime and violence prevention interventions. GIZ´s systemic approach focuses particularly on youth violence, given that young people under the age of 25 – typically the majority of the population in developing countries – are affected disproportionally by all types of violence. Logically, that means that involving young people is a crucial part in finding effective answers to achieving safety as is the involvement of those actors that have an influence on the behaviour of young people such as parents, teachers, social workers, etc. The GIZ systemic model is implemented through a workshop approach, which is elaborated in the "Handbook on the systemic prevention of youth violence." With interactive exercises, the workshop concept guides practitioners through a series of easy steps to plan for behavioural change among young people and relevant key actors. It helps in analyzing the context-specific causes and extent of youth violence as well as the life situation of young people. In this way prevention measures can be tailored according to the local context.
http://www.giz.de/Themen/de/31724.htm

Systemic approaches and collaborative action for realizing community safety

The ecological model:[5]

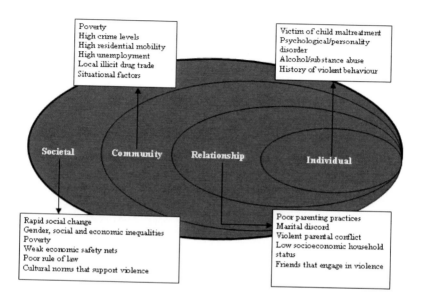

The WHO model not only helps to differentiate between the many and varied influencing factors behind violence and shows the relationships between individuals and their complex environment, but it also demonstrates the value and importance of collaborative action including various sectors and several levels in order to prevent violence. In South Africa, as much as in other violence hotspots around the world, where a whole variety of factors (enormous income disparities, poverty, social exclusion etc.) contribute to a fragile social system, it is all the more important to put an emphasis on systemic and inclusive approaches.

Crime and violence in South Africa

With approximately two million serious incidents of violent crime recorded every year, South Africa has one of the highest rates of violence in the world. Particularly striking in the South African context is the violent nature of crime. In multiple ways, crime and violence constantly undermine possibilities for the improvement of living conditions for most South Africans, impact negatively on people's ability to partake in social and economic life and erode citizens' trust in the state's capacity to provide safety as a public good.

---

[5] WHO, http://www.who.int/violenceprevention/approach/ecology/en/index.html

The root causes for this situation in the country are to be found in the legacy of the Apartheid system, which created physical (informal settlements, townships, homelands) and social disadvantages and exclusion for the great majority of the population. The often violent character of the conflict between the forces of liberation and the state has left an indelible mark on the nation's collective psyche that still has to be surmounted. Some commentators consequently refer to a "culture of violence" that pervades the society. Despite impressive developmental achievements since the transition to democracy eighteen years ago, intractable problems persist. According to the Gini coefficient, inequality has grown since the end of Apartheid, and the gap between rich and poor continues to be among the world's largest. High unemployment rates (officially around 25,5% of the economically active population is unemployed[6]) most acutely affect young people who constitute the majority of the population. Using the country's official definition of youth (15 to 35 years), about 34.5% of young people are currently unemployed. Of those who have jobs, a third earn less than $2 a day[7]. A generally poor education system (according to the World Economic Forum, South Africa ranks 132nd out of 144 countries for its primary education and 143rd in science and mathematics[8]) in combination with the break-down of family and community support structures in many areas have left too many young people with few perspectives and opportunities for personal growth and development. Further contributors to high rates of crime and violence are social norms that legitimise the use of violence, weak law enforcement as well as the continued social, economic and political marginalisation of women.

Responses to crime and violence

Since 1994, South Africa has put in place a host of progressive legislation, policies and structures at various levels to promote and enable more holistic and systemic approaches to creating safer communities. Among them are the 1996 National Crime Prevention Strategy and the 1998 White Paper on Safety and Security. More recently, the government has committed to the objective that '*all people in South Africa are and feel safe*' as one of its highest priorities. South Africa also has a relatively large and vibrant civil society sector, which has yielded a number of innovative interventions that address public safety in a holistic manner.

At the same time, in contradiction to official policy stances, there has been the tendency within government over the past decade to pursue a hard-line law-enforcement approach to crime and violence prevention, manifested for example in the re-militarisation of the police. This has served to undermine the focus on social crime prevention and more systemic approaches, which remain at the core of the solution to the problems of crime and violence facing the country.

---

[6] http://www.statssa.gov.za/keyindicators/keyindicators.asp

[7] The Economist: Sad South Africa. October 2012, from the print edition

[8] http://www3.weforum.org/docs/WEF_GlobalCompetitivenessReport_2012-13.pdf

The following three different case studies of interventions and methodologies illustrate the potential of collaborative action and systemic thinking in South Africa. These individual case studies represent only a small selection of what is being done at different levels and are not intended to present a collective approach. They are hugely varied in terms of the communities they involve and the complexities they are faced with. However, they all have in common that they take a systemic look at community safety.

Case study 1: Transforming fragile social systems- one community at a time

The Social Transformation System methodology developed by Dr. Barbara Holtmann aims to facilitate sustainable community safety, mobilizing key stakeholders in productive collaborations and to pave the way for more inclusive approaches. The methodology focuses on pro-social behaviour and community cohesion, delivering an optimistic vision rather than one based on fear of crime and violence. It is a methodology for local intervention by local actors. Acknowledging the need for practical solutions and local ownership, it recognizes that communities need to design and find their own destinies and collaborate with government and other stakeholders, such as donors, to build the protective layers that lead to resilience and more safety.

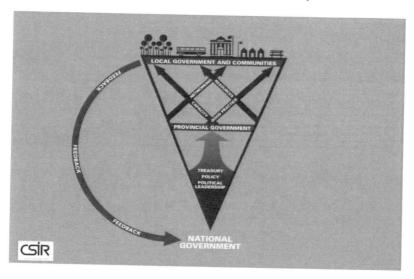

The need for local solutions: The "Upside-down three tiers of government" –model by Dr. Holtmann puts local government (and thus the people of South Africa) at the top of the inverted pyramid. In this model national government provides political leadership and guidance through policy and a legislative framework. The provincial level acts as an intermediate level which offers support, capacity building and guidance to local actors. The focus lies on the empowerment at the local level, where crime and violence are experienced most tangibly.

The methodology is applied in workshops which Dr. Holtmann conducts with institutions, service providers and communities all over South Africa. In the workshops participants are facilitated to use right brain thinking and intuitive knowledge to imagine the whole system in a transformed state, regardless of their individual mandates, interests or ability to influence parts of that system. The question then is, based on a shared understanding of the current flawed system, "what does it look like when it's fixed"? The jointly developed vision of "what it looks like when its fixed" acts as a benchmark against which the reality is then assessed and scored (indicators are scored on a four point scale - 4 is the ideal scenario; what it looks like when it's fixed, 3 is good, 2 is bad and 1 is terrible). This enables participants to rapidly evaluate the current status of the flawed system against their vision of the transformed system and provides essential insights into what needs to be done to fix it. The model demands that stakeholders each understand their usefulness to the transformation process and the supporting software programme also enables presentation of an individual stakeholder view, where only the elements to which a particular stakeholder are linked, are visible. This allows a stakeholder to manage collaborative partnerships, focusing on relationships of mutual inter-dependence.

During the interventions and implementation of various projects, participants can use the software system and input data they collect as part of their work. The software then acts as a live data feed, where participants can log on and assess areas of weakness or strength, in relation to the greater system. This also helps to measure impact over time and illustrates how the system as a whole moves towards transformation as a consequence of targeted collaborative actions.

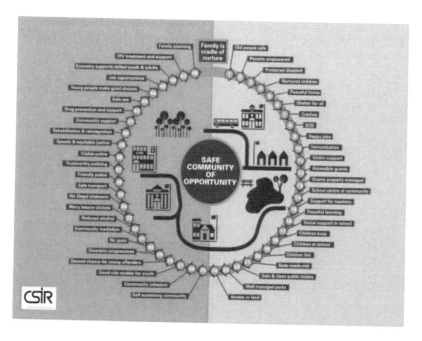

What it looks like when it's fixed - the safe community of opportunity model by Dr. Barbara Holtmann

The model requires individual and collective accountability; it highlights inter-dependence and offers pragmatic motivations for partnership and integrated approaches. It provides also a platform for joint planning and the development of inclusive strategies and is thus also a useful example of how systemic approaches can be very pragmatically translated into concrete preventative interventions that speak to the challenges in the communities. This methodology was for instance applied within the development process of a local crime prevention strategy for the Central Karoo District Municipality, a rural and largely deprived region in South Africa. The research team began by asking people to imagine 'what it looks like when it's fixed'. In groups of varying composition, participants were asked to paint or draw images of a safe Central Karoo. From the elements that made up the images, they identified the key activists and actions that would be required to achieve a safe community and build sustainable resilience.

Case study 2: Johannesburg's City Safety Programme

The local level is the level where government, civil society, the business community and citizens interact most tangibly, which implies there are ample opportunities for citizen's participation and inclusive approaches. The role of local/city government in

South Africa directly in crime prevention is limited. However, within their legislated mandate, municipalities are able to invest in public safety through interventions such as community development, urban design and management, protection of vulnerable groups, infrastructure upgrades and by-law enforcement. These all require a high level of collaboration between municipal departments and other actors. The potential of such integrated approaches on the city/local level is demonstrated by a number of success stories in South Africa, one of which is the "Jo'burg City Safety Programme" (JCSP).

Johannesburg has a reputation has one of the world's most violent cities. The establishment of the JCSP was triggered by the urgent need for more of the city's departments to better understand their roles and to assume responsibility with respect to enhancing safety in the city. Through the programme, safety promotion and crime prevention are tackled from a variety of standpoints by a larger pool of role-players, thus addressing the problem more quickly and effectively. The JCSP has successfully pioneered a new and innovative way to address crime by moving away from the prevailing "silo" mentality to an integrated way of working in the public sector. The programme provides the platform for all the city role-players in a particular focal area to meet regularly with the South African Police Service (SAPS) and other provincial role-players, to discuss ways in which their work impacts on each others' work and on overall safety aspects. In so doing, city departments, enforcement agencies and municipal-owned entities are able to develop joint solutions to safety challenges. The programme has also developed the capacity of city departments to proactively consider topics such as urban safety/service delivery problems that impact on public safety in the city.

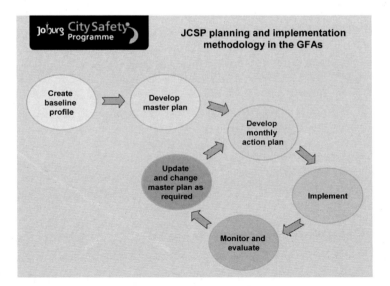

Figure 1 : JCSP Methodology

Another factor that contributed greatly to the success of the JCSP was that the programme deliberately sought to improve the coordination with provincial role-players to increase leverage. This is absolutely vital to creating more holistic programmes as all three spheres of government (local, provincial, national) have differing but complementary roles and responsibilities in the creation of safer cities and communities. Unfortunately, the lack of collaboration between the different levels of government is also one of the persistent challenges in South Africa, which makes it sometimes difficult to ensure stringent policy implementation and effective service delivery at the local level. Since its introduction, the JCSP has contributed to significant decreases in crime and violence in Johannesburg. For example, between 2003 and 2011, the number of murders has decreased by 30%, attempted murders by 50% and contact crimes by 27%.

Lessons Learned from the JSCP

- Strong support from the local government political leadership is a precondition;
- Interdepartmental understanding of their role in urban safety is essential;
- Holistic approach to issues of safety at city level is an essential ingredient to drive and orient crime-prevention initiatives
- Inter and intra-departmental cooperation and coordination is paramount

---

Case study 3: The provincial Department of Community Safety in the Western Cape Province

One of the provinces in South Africa that provides a good example of what can be achieved through coordinated and collaborative approaches is the Western Cape. With the introduction of the provincial Transversal Management System the Western Cape government is proactively tackling the problem of different departments all operating in isolation, not communicating with each other and often working within the same communities unaware of the others' programmes and action plans. In the past this resulted in a fragmented state of affairs and a duplication of efforts, to the detriment of service delivery. The new governance model that has been introduced is now more customized for the particular needs of the people of the Western Cape. The provincial Transversal Management System is designed to achieve measurable outcomes for target communities, through a focus on sectors rather than singular departments. In other words, sectoral clusters address issues transversally while line departments become the implementing agents. One strategic key issue that is being addressed within the sectoral clusters is how to increase safety.

The Western Cape Provincial Government's Department of Community Safety has long embraced integrated and holistic approaches to crime prevention and safety, based on the recognition that crime cannot be addressed through law enforcement alone. It has thus formulated the strategic goal "*to make every community in the province a safe place in which to live, work, learn, relax and move about.*"

One of the main pillars of the department's safety strategy is to establish civilian oversight mechanisms for policing in the province. This is being done due to the fact that despite a clear oversight and monitoring mandate in respect of South African Police Service (SAPS) activities and functions within their area of jurisdiction, provinces have not done enough to develop and implement systematic and sustainable oversight or monitoring mechanisms. Functions normally associated with effective oversight, such as the independent collection of data, the regular evaluation of performance at station level and the development of measurable performance standards are not being sufficiently implemented, despite provinces having a clear mandate to do so. In an effort to addressing this issue, the Western Cape Government drafted the Community Safety Bill, currently put out for public comment. The main focus of the Bill is to clarify and articulate the powers, functions and duties of the provincial government as it relates to overseeing policing. It also sets out to create systems of integrated safety information that is partly based on innovative ways to collect data, such as participatory safety audits, as opposed to total reliance on crime statistics. In addition, it intends to institutionalize a system that draws information from morbidity and non-fatal injury data. The rationale for this is based on the understanding that crime statistics often remain a poor indicator of safety and that a more comprehensive information base is needed when considering safety needs.

A further important pillar of the Western Cape's crime prevention strategy is the creation of partnerships. In support of an inclusive "whole of society" approach and in recognizing that safety cannot be achieved without an integrated approach, the province aims to set-up and strengthen existing partnerships with various role-players, including but not limited to business, NGOs and other organs of civil society. The establishment of a partnership entity outside of government, which is aimed at creating an "*incubator*" capacity, is envisaged. One of the main purposes of the envisaged entity will be to identify programmes and projects which add maximum value to increasing safety in the Western Cape, thereby creating opportunities for enhanced collaboration and joint action. Along this line, the so-called provincial Transversal Management System has created institutionalized, cross-departmental working groups under its strategic objectives on selected issues such as injury prevention, safety or criminality and gangs.

Inclusive Violence and Crime Prevention- GIZ's contribution in South Africa

Despite innovative initiatives and interventions such as the three presented case studies, South Africa's response to the country's inclination towards violence and crime has in recent years been largely dominated by a rigid law enforcement approach. The necessary shift from a security-based approach to a notion of safety[9] is only slowly gaining traction. However, with the new vision for community safety contained in the National Development Plan, the prospect now exists for a renewed government commitment to a broader, systemic approach to safety, as originally envisaged in the 1996 National Crime Prevention Strategy.

Among the key challenges to be dealt with is the struggling culture of collaboration across sectors, institutions as well as between public-, civil society- and community-based organisations in their attempts at preventing violence and increasing the safety of citizens. There are also insufficient opportunities for sharing knowledge, skills and experience between multiple disciplines such as urban development, youth- and social work, economic empowerment, preventive police work and community policing, to name but a few. Lastly, few avenues exist for further training and skills building for violence and crime prevention across the range of relevant sectors, and the majority of government programmes and processes have yet to integrate a safety lens.

Against this backdrop, German Development Cooperation (GIZ) on behalf of the Federal Ministry for Economic Cooperation and Development (BMZ), and with local partners, is currently implementing the "Inclusive Violence and Crime Prevention for Safe Public Spaces (VCP)" programme as part of its overall support in the area of governance and administration in South Africa. Drawing on GIZ's systemic approach to violence prevention, the project specifically aims to enable governmental and non-governmental actors to jointly develop and implement innovative measures that increase the safety of residents, particularly young people, in selected sites. Further, it addresses the implementation challenge of South Africa's progressive national policies at the level local governance. Part of this is to support local government to realise its role in creating an enabling environment for the co-production of safer communities, based on the notion of safety as a public good. Another aspect of the programme is to provide more opportunities for different professional groups to get further training in violence prevention and to create platforms for knowledge sharing and networking, so that all the good local initiatives that exist in the country can learn from and infuse each other.

Conclusion

The different initiatives discussed in this paper, although quite different in their nature and scope, point in the same direction, highlighting that change is possible but

---

[9] "security"- protection against a perceived or known threat
"safety" - absence of threat and fear

inevitably depends on change, a change that enables more collaborative and holistic approaches. The cases illustrate that a safer South Africa is achievable, where actors understand their respective mandates and combine them in joint safety approaches.

The manner in which the Provincial Government of the Western Cape as well as the Jo'burg City Safety Programme are addressing the challenges of crime and violence within their territory provide promising examples for other provinces and cities to learn from. They both demonstrate that comprehensive approaches that look at the root causes of violence, rather than purely focusing on the symptoms, are a cost-effective, sustainable and sensible way forward when it comes to creating safety. Models and practical applications such as Barbara Holtmanns Social Transformation System can assist governmental and non-governmental actors to face the often overwhelmingly complex challenges in the creation of safer environments and add value to their interventions through providing a foundation on which to plan for change. Change on the scale required by a society suffering broad and deep vulnerability cannot be achieved through simple, linear interventions by one or a few sectors. It requires an understanding of the complexities, an appetite for true prevention, inclusive collaboration and a shared sense of purpose to transform the fragility and vulnerability into sustainable resilience.

References:

Deutsche Gesellschaft für Internationale Zusammenarbeit (GIZ GmbH: Systemic Prevention of Youth Violence: A handbook to design and plan comprehensive violence prevention measures. 2011.
Dr. Holtmann, Barbara: What it looks like when it's fixed. PWC, 2011.
International Centre for the Prevention of Crime (ICPC): Crime Prevention and Community Safety: International Report 2012. (P. 123 – 134). 2012.
National Planning Commission South Africa: National Development Plan: Vision for 2030. (P. 349 – 363). 2011.
National Crime Prevention Strategy South Africa. Policy Paper, 1996
The Economist: Sad South Africa. October 2012, from the print edition
The Economist: Over the rainbow. October 2012, from the print edition
World Bank: Country Assessment on Youth Violence, Policy and Programmes in South Africa. June 2012.

http://www.who.int/violenceprevention/approach/ecology/en/index.html
http://www.saps.gov.za/statistics/reports/crimestats/2012/crime_stats.htm
http://www.statssa.gov.za/keyindicators/keyindicators.asp
http://www.unhabitat.org/pmss/listItemDetails.aspx?publicationID=3387

Alexander Butchart

Preventing Violence: an Overview

The World Health Organization (WHO) mandate is to advance the attainment by all peoples of the highest possible level of health. WHO supports Member States to design, implement and monitor science-based prevention programming and service provision, and the Organization's agenda is set by the World Health Assembly (WHA). In 1996 and 1997, the WHA adopted resolutions calling on WHO to develop normative guidance on a public health approach to the prevention of violence, and to assist Member States in developing, implementing, and evaluating violence prevention policies and programmes. In 2002 WHO published the *World report on violence and health* (Krug et al, 2002) the first-ever comprehensive state-of-the-science review of violence and violence prevention. This was followed in 2003 by a second WHA resolution on implementing the recommendations of the *World report on violence and health*. Since then WHO has continued to produce normative guidance on violence prevention; to advocate at global and regional levels for increased investment in prevention, and to provide support for country-level activities.

Underlying WHO's involvement in the prevention of violence is the recognition that while violence is most often seen as a problem for the criminal justice sector to address (which of course it is), violence is also a health problem. Health care systems deal with victims of violence; violence has many long-term, far-reaching consequences for mental, physical and reproductive health, and the public health sector is explicitly set up to support prevention activities. By definition, public health is not about individual patients. Its focus is on dealing with diseases and with conditions and problems affecting health, and it aims to provide the maximum benefit for the largest number of people. This does not mean that public health ignores the care of individuals. Rather, the concern is to prevent health problems, and to extend better care and safety to entire populations (Dahlberg and Krug, 2002).

Defining and Categorizing Violence

WHO defines violence as "the intentional use of power, threatened or actual, against oneself, another person or against a group or community, that either results in or has a high likelihood of resulting in injury, death, psychological harm, maldevelopment or deprivation" (Dahlberg and Krug, 2002). Three general types of violence are encompassed by this definition: interpersonal, self-directed, and collective. Interpersonal violence includes forms perpetrated by an individual or small group of individuals, such as child maltreatment by parents and caregivers (Runyan et al, 2002), youth violence (Mercy et al, 2002), intimate partner violence (Heise et al., 2002), sexual violence (Jewkes et al, 2002), and elder maltreatment (Wolf et al., 2002). Self-directed violence includes suicidal behaviour and self-abuse where the intent may not be to take one's own life (Deleo et al. 2002). Collective violence is the use of violence by groups or individuals who identify themselves as members of a group, against another group or set of individuals, to achieve political, social, or economic objectives. It includes war, terrorism, and state-sponsored violence towards its own citizens (Zwi et al. 2002). These types of violence can involve physical, sexual, and psychological abuse, as well as deprivation or neglect.

Magnitude and Consequences

Globally, it is estimated that 1.51 million people per year die due to violence (WHO GBD 2008). This is almost as many as the number of deaths due to HIV/AIDS, somewhat more than the totals for tuberculosis and road traffic injuries, and nearly twice that for malaria. Of all 1.51 million deaths each year due to violence, half (782,000) are due to suicide, a third (535,000) are homicides, and 12% (182,000) a direct result of war. WHO focuses on understanding and preventing interpersonal violence, while recognizing and addressing the links between this and the other main types of violence.

All forms of violence, but especially child maltreatment, intimate partner violence and sexual violence contribute significantly to depression, sexually transmitted diseases and unwanted pregnancies, while also increasing the likelihood of engaging in risky behaviours, such as unsafe sex, smoking and the harmful use of alcohol and drugs (e.g. Felitti et al, 1998; Norman et al, 2012). Via these behaviours, they can lead to cancers, cardiovascular diseases, diabetes, liver disease and other chronic diseases.

Public Health Approach to Violence Prevention

WHO's public health approach to violence prevention perspective is set out in the 2002 *World report on violence and health* (Krug et al, 2002) and companion volumes that provide technical guidance on implementing its recommendations (see Box 1), and on the prevention of specific subtypes of violence (e.g. child maltreatment, youth violence, and intimate partner and sexual violence), all of which are freely available online at WHO's violence prevention website http://www.who.int/violence_injury_prevention/publications/violence/en/index.html). The public health approach to dealing with violence is population-based. It emphasizes primary prevention – doing something about the problem before it occurs. It draws on a wide range of expertise across many sectors, and it is based in science. It asserts that everything – from identifying the problem, to planning, testing and evaluating responses – should be based on sound research and informed by the best evidence.

> **Box 1. World report on violence and health recommendations**
>
> The *World report on violence and health* (Krug et al, 2002) and the 2003 World Health Assembly resolution 56.4 make nine recommendations, which are to:
>
> 1. Create, implement and monitor a national action plan for violence prevention.
> 2. Enhance capacity for collecting data on violence.
> 3. Define priorities for, and support research on, the causes, consequences, costs and prevention of violence.
> 4. Promote primary prevention responses.
> 5. Strengthen responses for victims of violence.
> 6. Integrate violence prevention into social and educational policies, and thereby promote gender and social equality.
> 7. Increase collaboration and exchange of information on violence prevention.
> 8. Promote and monitor adherence to international treaties, laws and other mechanisms to protect human rights.
> 9. Seek practical, internationally agreed responses to the global drugs trade and the global arms trade.

In moving from problem to response, the public health approach has four steps. The first step is to statistically describe and monitor the extent of the problem to identify the groups and communities at risk. The next step is to identify and understand the factors that place people at risk for violence – to assess which factors may also be amenable to intervention. The third step is to develop and evaluate interventions to reduce these risks, and the fourth step is to implement and apply widely the prevention strategies that are found to work.

The public health approach adopts an ecological model for understanding the causes, consequences and prevention of violence (see Figure 1). The ecological model is based on evidence that no single factor can explain why some people or groups are at higher risk of interpersonal violence while others are more protected from it. Instead, the model views interpersonal violence as the outcome of interaction among factors at four levels: the individual, the relationship, the community, and the societal. In this model, the interaction between factors at the different levels is just as important as the influence of factors within a single level. For example, longitudinal studies suggest that complications associated with pregnancy and delivery, perhaps because they lead to neurological damage and psychological or personality disorder (individual risk factors), seem to predict violence in youth and young adulthood mainly when they occur in combination with other problems within the family (a close relationship factor), such as poor parenting practices.

Figure 1. Ecological model showing shared risk factors for sub-types of interpersonal violence (adapted from Dahlberg and Krug, 2002)

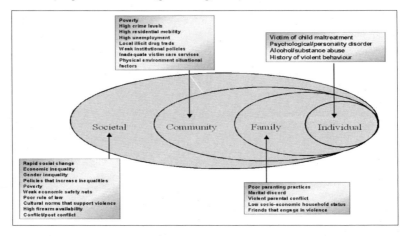

Among the risk factors for the different types of interpersonal violence, some are common to most sub-types, and Figure 1 lists some of these crosscutting risk factors at each of the four levels of the ecological model. At the individual level, personal history and biological factors influence how individuals behave and increase their likelihood of becoming a victim or a perpetrator of violence. Among these factors are being a victim of child maltreatment, psychological or personality disorders, alcohol and/or substance abuse, and a history of behaving aggressively or having experienced abuse. Personal relationships such as family, friends, intimate partners, and peers may influence the risks of becoming a victim or perpetrator of violence. For example, having violent friends may influence whether a young person engages in or becomes a victim of violence. Community contexts in which social relationships occur, such as schools, neighbourhoods and workplaces, also influence violence. Risk factors here may include the level of unemployment, population density, mobility, and the existence of a local drug or gun trade. Societal factors influence whether violence is encouraged or inhibited. These include economic and social policies that maintain socioeconomic inequalities between people, the availability of firearms and other weapons, and social and cultural norms such as those around male dominance over women, parental dominance over children, and cultural norms that endorse violence as an acceptable method to resolve conflicts.

Violence Prevention Strategies

The publication *Violence prevention: the evidence* (WHO and Liverpool John Moore's University [LJMU], 2009, a-h) clusters the scientific evidence for violence prevention into seven strategies (WHO and LJMU, 2009, a-g), and within each strategy reviews the evidence for the effectiveness of specific interventions. The prevention strategies selected are scientifically credible; include interventions at each of the four ecological levels; can potentially reduce multiple forms of violence, and represent areas where developing countries and funding agencies can make reasonable investments. The seven violence prevention strategies are:

1. Developing safe, stable and nurturing relationships between children and their parents and caregivers (WHO and LJMU, 2009, a);
2. Developing life skills in children and adolescents (WHO and LJMU, 2009, b);
3. Reducing the availability and harmful use of alcohol (WHO and LJMU, 2009, c);
4. Reducing access to guns, knives and pesticides (WHO and LJMU, 2009, d);
5. Promoting gender equality to prevent violence against women (WHO and LJMU, 2009, e);
6. Changing cultural and social norms that support violence (WHO and LJMU, 2009, f;
7. Victim identification, care and support programmes (WHO and LJMU, 2009, g).

An eighth briefing in the series provides an overview of the main findings for each of the seven strategies, showing which of the different types of violence each strategy has been shown to impact (WHO and LJMU, 2009, h).

Developing safe, stable and nurturing relationships between children and their parents or caregivers

Interventions under this strategy are those that deliver early, primary prevention services to avoid the development of child maltreatment and childhood aggression. They include parent training programmes; providing information and support for parents, and parent and child programmes (e.g. providing preschool education, family support and child/health services). The evidence shows that the ability of parenting programmes and parent and child programmes to reduce child maltreatment and aggressive behaviours in youth is well supported by evidence. One of the best examples of a parenting programme is the Nurse Family Partnership in the USA, a home visiting programme that reduced child maltreatment by 48% (see WHO and Liverpool John Moores University, 2009, a).

Developing life skills in children and adolescents

Interventions that aim to develop life skills in children and adolescents provide cognitive, emotional, interpersonal and social skills to enable children and youth to deal with the challenges of everyday life. They include preschool enrichment programmes that provide skills to children before they enter formal education and may focus on parenting education for adults; social development training in skills such as empathy, communication in relationships, conflict resolution, and anger management, and vocational training, by providing at risk youth with skills to find work. There is some evidence showing that preschool enrichment and social development programmes can reduce aggression and improve social skills, particularly in at-risk children. For instance, an outcome evaluation study from South Korea showed that both social skills training for the children and parent education were highly effective in reducing aggressive behaviour among young children and in fostering positive parenting behaviours (see WHO and LJMU, 2009, b).

Reducing the availability and harmful use of alcohol

Strategies for preventing violence by reducing the availability and harmful use of alcohol include regulating alcohol availability through sales times and restrictions on outlet density, and raising alcohol prices, through taxation and minimum pricing. That alcohol-focused interventions can reduce violence is supported by emerging evidence. However, there are barriers to intervening - including commercial interests - and there are few high-quality studies. One example of an effective intervention is a ban on sales of alcohol sales between 11pm and 6am in Diadema, Brazil, which led to a 44% decrease in homicides, and a decrease in injuries resulting from intimate partner violence (see WHO and LJMU, 2009, c).

Reducing access to guns, knives and pesticides

Reducing access to lethal means – such as guns, knives and pesticides – can help to prevent violence and reduce the severity of its consequences. Strategies that show promise here include strengthening legislation through weapons bans and licensing schemes, and increasing the enforcement of legislation, such as test purchasing to identify illegal sales of weapons, and police stop and search measures. One example is from Colombia, where local legislation in Bogota and Cali banned the carrying of firearms on holidays, weekends after paydays, and election days. Studies showed that the incidence of homicides in both cities was lower on days when the ban was in place compared to similar days when people were allowed to carry guns (see WHO and LJMU, 2009, d).

Promoting gender equality to prevent violence against women

Interventions that promote gender equality include schools-based interventions to address gender norms and attitudes, including programmes to prevent dating violence, and community interventions such as microfinance programmes combined with gender equity training. Schools-based programmes to prevent dating violence are well supported by evidence, and community-based interventions are supported by emerging evidence, but much more high quality research is needed in this area, especially from developing countries. One well-evaluated example is the Intervention with Microfinance and Gender Equity programme – or IMAGE - in South Africa. After the programme, women from villages where IMAGE was implemented reported 50% fewer acts of intimate partner violence than in similar villages where IMAGE was not implemented (see WHO and LJMU, 2009, e).

Changing cultural and social norms that support violence

Interventions for changing cultural and social norms are aimed at challenging expectations that support violent behaviour, and include mass media campaigns to provide messages on health behaviour to a wide audience, and edutainment; social norms and marketing programmes that target specific groups and aim to correct misperceptions of cultural norms, and enacting and enforcing laws and policies that make violent behaviour an offence. There is limited evidence for most interventions in this area due to a lack of research on their effects, so a priority is to do more rigorous evaluations, in particular studies that use actual violence as an outcome. One programme that has been evaluated - Soul City, again in South Africa – led to a reduction in the acceptance of intimate partner violence, and a strengthened belief that such violence could be prevented (see WHO and LJMU, 2009, f).

Victim identification, care and support programmes

The impact of violence can be reduced, and revenge attacks and re-victimization prevented, through victim identification, care and support programmes such as screening and referral programmes to identify and support victims of violence, and advocacy support programmes that provide support and guidance to victims, e.g. counselling, education, legal aid. There is some good evidence for the use of advocacy support programmes, and promising evidence for screening and referral, psychosocial interventions, and protection orders. For example, for every dollar invested in Child Advocacy Centers in the USA, over US$3 were saved in support services and costs on investigations. These centres offer enhanced multi-disciplinary services for abused children all in one location (see WHO and LJMU, 2009, g).

WHO Global Campaign for Violence Prevention

The WHO Global Campaign for Violence Prevention serves as the main platform for encouraging implementation by countries of the *World report on violence and health* recommendations, and the seven violence prevention strategies described above. The Global Campaign for Violence Prevention also provides a platform for collaboration and the exchange of information between actors at global and country level. This platform is the Violence Prevention Alliance (VPA), a network of WHO Member States, international and national agencies and civil society organizations working to prevent violence.

Through the Global Campaign, the *World report on violence and health* has had national launches in 50 countries, 25 national reports on violence and health have been published, and a wide range of regional- and country-level activities initiated. These efforts have resulted in a steadily increasing country-level demand for WHO to provide technical support for the development of prevention policies and programmes. Central to meeting this demand is the assistance provided by VPA participants, who play a key role in advancing the local implementation of WHO global recommendations and guidance. Also central to the Global Campaign for Violence Prevention is the *Global status report on violence prevention*, by which WHO, with UNDP and UNODC, is surveying all Member States to obtain baseline information on violence prevention policies, data collection mechanisms; laws and prevention programmes, and victim services.

Regional- and Country-level Activities

The recommendations of the 2002 *World report on violence and health;* subsequent guidance on preventing child maltreatment and violence against women, and the seven strategies described in *Violence prevention: the evidence* (WHO and LJMU, 2009, a-h) have become the backbone of violence prevention policies and programmes in thousands of settings. Well over half of all WHO Member States have officially appointed Ministry of Health focal points for violence prevention. WHO provides technical support for prevention programmes in an increasing number of countries. Five out of six WHO regional offices – the Americas; Africa; Europe; South East Asia and, in October 2012, the Western Pacific – have adopted violence prevention resolutions, and several regions publish periodic reports on violence and violence prevention in their Member States.

Violence Prevention Alliance

The VPA is an informal network of governmental, non-governmental, international and private organizations. It aims to implement the nine recommendations of the *World report on violence and health*, and its participants are committed to the public health approach to violence prevention. The VPA was established at the first Milestones of a Global Campaign for Violence Prevention Meeting in January 2004, and as of January 2013 its membership stands at just over 50 participants. All participants actively support international violence prevention efforts, and they include, the United Nations Development Fund; the United Nations Office on Drugs and Crime; the International Center for the Prevention of Crime, the German Congress on Crime Prevention, and the Open Society Institute's Preventing violence and crime initiative. VPA strategic priorities for 2011-2015 include strengthening intersectoral collaboration for violence prevention; reinforcing the VPA as a network of networks; mobilizing resources for the VPA and for the field of violence prevention; contributing to violence prevention capacity building, and defining an international violence prevention research agenda. To achieve these aims, the VPA works through several project groups, including on parenting for child maltreatment prevention, criminal justice liaison, and research.

Another key mechanism by which the VPA is working to enhance coherence between different international violence prevention stakeholders is the *Plan of action for the Global Campaign for Violence Prevention for the period 2012-2020* (VPA, 2012). This aims to unify the efforts of the main actors in international violence prevention and identify a small set of priorities for the field, by presenting six national level goals towards which efforts can be directed. These are closely tied to the *World report on violence and health* recommendations, and the evidence base for violence prevention. The first two goals aim to prioritize violence prevention within the global public health agenda; the next three aim to build strong foundations for on-going violence prevention efforts; and the last aims to promote the implementation of evidence-informed violence prevention strategies on parenting, life-skills, social norms, alcohol, the risks of firearm-related deaths and injuries, and services for victims. The objective of the Campaign in the coming years is to support the achievement of these goals in countries around the world. The target audience for the Plan of Action is the global violence prevention community, including governments, United Nations and official development assistance agencies, philanthropic foundations, nongovernmental organizations and academic institutions.

Global Status Report on Violence Prevention

To measure violence prevention efforts in Member States, WHO, with UNDP and UNODC, is preparing a *Global status report on violence prevention*. This report will evaluate the extent to which countries have been implementing the recommendations of the *World report on violence and health*. It will focus on child maltreatment, youth violence, intimate partner violence, sexual violence, and elder maltreatment. This snapshot of the state of interpersonal violence prevention in each country will serve as a benchmark for countries to assess their violence prevention efforts; a baseline to track future progress in violence prevention internationally; to identify gaps in national responses to violence that need to be addressed, and a catalyst for further prevention action by countries. Data collection will begin in 2013. In each country, a National Data Coordinator will collect data from violence prevention respondents from different sectors including justice, law enforcement/police, interior, education, gender and women, relevant non-governmental organizations, and research institutions. These respondents will then come together as a multi-sectoral consensus panel and provide one set of data that best represents the situation in their country. Following official government endorsement of the completed questionnaires, the data will be collated and analyzed to provide input for the *Global status report on violence prevention*. The *Global status report on violence prevention* will be launched in late 2014.

Discussion and Conclusion

While much has been achieved over the last decade by way of increased awareness about the importance of preventing violence using a science-based approach, progress by type of violence and country income level is uneven. For all types of interpersonal violence, low-income countries are still at the stage of needing to define the problem, and many still lack cause of death registration systems that would allow them to track violence-related deaths. Except for elder maltreatment, middle-income countries are mostly at the point where they are using their local knowledge of causes and risk factors to identify prevention strategies that work in their own settings. High-income countries are scaling up child maltreatment and youth violence prevention, but are still at the point of identifying and evaluating effective prevention strategies for intimate partner and sexual violence, and maltreatment.

References

Dahlberg LL, Krug EG. Violence – a global public health problem. In: Krug E, Dahlberg LL, Mercy JA, Zwi AB, Lozano R, eds. World Report on Violence and Health. Geneva, Switzerland: World Health Organization; 2002:3-21.

Deleo D, Bertolote J, Lester D. Self-Directed Violence. In: Krug E, Dahlberg LL, Mercy JA, Zwi AB, Lozano R, eds. World Report on Violence and Health. Geneva, Switzerland: World Health Organization; 2002:185-212.

Felitti VJ, Anda RF, Nordenberg D, Williamson DF, Spitz AM, Edwards V, Koss MP, Marks, JS. The relationship of adult health status to childhood abuse and household dysfunction. American Journal of Preventive Medicine, 1998;14:245–258.

Heise L, Garcia-Moreno C. Violence by intimate partners. In: Krug E, Dahlberg LL, Mercy JA, Zwi AB, Lozano R, eds. World Report on Violence and Health. Geneva, Switzerland: World Health Organization; 2002:87–121.

Jewkes R, Sen P, Garcia-Moreno C. Sexual violence. In: Krug E, Dahlberg LL, Mercy JA, Zwi AB, Lozano R, eds. World Report on Violence and Health. Geneva, Switzerland: World Health Organization; 2002:149-181.

Krug E, Dahlberg LL, Mercy JA, Zwi AB, Lozano R, eds. World Report on Violence and Health. Geneva, Switzerland: World Health Organization; 2002.

Mercy JA, Butchart A. Farrington D, Cerda M. Youth violence. In: Krug E, Dahlberg LL, Mercy JA, Zwi AB, Lozano R, eds. World Report on Violence and Health. Geneva, Switzerland: World Health Organization; 2002:23–56.

Mercy JA, Krug EG, Dahlberg LL, Zwi AB. Violence and health: The United States in a global perspective. American Journal of Public Health 2003;93(2):256-61.

Norman RE, Byambaa M, De R, Butchart A, Scott J, et al. (2012) The Long-Term Health Consequences of Child Physical Abuse, Emotional Abuse, and Neglect: A Systematic Review and Meta-Analysis. PLoS Med 9(11): e1001349. doi:10.1371/journal.pmed.1001349

Runyan D, Wattam C, Ikeda R, Hassan F, Ramiro L. Child abuse and neglect by parents and other caregivers. In: Krug E, Dahlberg LL, Mercy JA, Zwi AB, Lozano R, eds. World Report on Violence and Health. Geneva, Switzerland: World Health Organization; 2002:59-86.

WHO Global Burden of Disease (GBD) mortality database for 2008. http://www.who.int/gho/mortality_burden_disease/en/

WHO and Liverpool John Moores University (LJMU). Violence prevention: the evidence. Developing safe, stable and nurturing relationships between children and their parents and caregivers. Geneva: WHO, 2009, a)

WHO and Liverpool John Moores University (LJMU). Violence prevention: the evidence. Preventing violence by developing life skills in children and adolescents. Geneva: WHO, 2009, b)

WHO and Liverpool John Moores University (LJMU). Violence prevention: the evidence. Preventing violence by reducing the availability and harmful use of alcohol. Geneva: WHO, 2009, c)
WHO and Liverpool John Moores University (LJMU). Violence prevention: the evidence. Guns, knives and pesticides: reducing aces to lethal means. Geneva: WHO, 2009, d)
WHO and Liverpool John Moores University (LJMU). Violence prevention: the evidence. Promoting gender equality to prevent violence against women. Geneva: WHO, 2009, e)
WHO and Liverpool John Moores University (LJMU). Violence prevention: the evidence. Changing cultural and social norms that prevent violence. Geneva: WHO, 2009, f)
WHO and Liverpool John Moores University (LJMU). Violence prevention: the evidence. Reducing violence through victim identification, care and support programmes. Geneva: WHO, 2009, g)
WHO and Liverpool John Moores University (LJMU). Violence prevention: the evidence. Overview. Geneva: WHO, 2009, h)
Violence Prevention Alliance [VPA]. Global campaign for violence prevention: plan of action for 2012-2020. Geneva: VPA, 2012.
Wolf R, Daichman L, Bennett G. Abuse of the elderly. In: Krug E, Dahlberg LL, Mercy JA, Zwi AB, Lozano R, eds. World Report on Violence and Health. Geneva, Switzerland: World Health Organization; 2002:125-145.
Zwi AB, Garfield R, Loretti A. Collective violence. In: Krug E, Dahlberg LL, Mercy JA, Zwi AB, Lozano R, eds. World Report on Violence and Health. Geneva, Switzerland: World Health Organization; 2002:213–239.

German Congress on Crime Prevention and Congress Partners

Munich Declaration of the 17th German Congress on Crime Prevention

Munich, 16 and 17 April 2012

Security in Urban and Rural Society

"Security in Urban and Rural Society" refers to far more than domestic and national security. Equally vital is social and financial security, in which reliability and planning certainty are given. This is, however, something that can no longer be taken for granted in modern society. While fundamental social change brings opportunity, it also brings risk. This is a situation that must not be allowed to result in social inequality or the associated destabilisation of personal lives. Ensuring social security by ensuring social equality is not only a basic human need – it is also a complex state responsibility that must be tackled using holistic prevention measures.

This is why the 17th German Congress on Crime Prevention (GCOCP) shines the spotlight on security. In line with the findings of Dr. Wiebke Steffen's expert report, "Sicherheit als Grundbedürfnis der Menschen und Staatliche Aufgabe" (Security as a Basic Human Need and as a State Responsibility), the GCOCP and its congress partners – DBH-Bildungswerk, the State of Bavaria, the City of Munich, the German Police Crime Prevention Programme (Pro PK), and the WEISSER RING victim support organisation – hereby publish this **Munich Declaration**:

1. The social state as the basis for social justice

*As a social and welfare state, the Federal Republic of Germany has created the necessary constitutional framework in which to alleviate the impact of social disintegration, even out social inequalities, provide social security and justice, and foster social cohesion. The **German Congress on Crime Prevention** therefore urges policymakers to adhere to the principle of the **social state** as enshrined in the German Basic Law. Socially just policy must provide opportunities for financial and social participation and achievement for all. Each and every individual should within the scope of their personal freedom be able to lead an independent life in which they participate broadly in society.*

*Effective **poverty prevention** plays a key role: Poverty is a barrier to social participation and independent living.*

*If social prevention is to be used to alleviate income, education and integration poverty, then greater focus must be placed our **cities, towns and rural communities**, and they must be given all the support they need – all the more so given the large regional* *disparities along all dimensions of social justice. And to be effective, the prevention measures implemented must be tailored to local needs at local level.*

2. Social security and domestic security: Social policy as opposed to crime policy

The **German Congress on Crime Prevention** *urges policymakers to address social fears and anxieties, to define and communicate them in their own right, and to reject the 'punitive turn' seen in other countries. Instead, the CGOCP asks that policymakers continue to address economic and social policy-related uncertainties via social policy rather than exclusively by means of crime policy. Political discourse on this subject has been remarkably restrained to date; this should remain the case and serve as an example for both the media and some parts of the academic discourse.*

While good social policy can reduce both crime and fear of crime, the **German Congress on Crime Prevention** *expressly warns against calls for social policy to be used as crime prevention policy. The CGOCP reiterates its call for a narrow definition of crime prevention which defines as 'crime preventive' only those strategies, models and measures aimed directly or indirectly at preventing or reducing crime.*

The **German Congress on Crime Prevention** *points to the portion of crime prevention which has led neither to a 'punitive turn' in Germany nor to the creation of an 'American-style' security society, but which instead has remained and should remain a policy of domestic security which trusts in the mechanisms of integration and educationalisation integral to a social and welfare state. On the one hand, this can be done by ensuring that prevention receives priority over repression when preventing or reducing crime. On the other, where repression is necessary, it can be done by acknowledging education and resocialisation as important functions of punishment. Both underline the notion of and the need for inclusion and social participation.*

3. Crime prevention must focus on local, social and cultural contexts

The **German Congress on Crime Prevention** *calls for critical analysis of the risks of misconceived crime prevention. Crime prevention must be understood in a narrow sense in order to avoid social policy issues being addressed exclusively by means of crime policy. In all crime prevention programmes, projects and measures, careful problem and cause analysis at local level should be carried out to look at the local, social and cultural aspects of crime and then justify the need for and test the effectiveness of the crime prevention measures involved.*

If crime prevention is both interpreted and implemented in this way, then the **German Congress on Crime Prevention** *believes it can contribute to alleviating uncertainties and exclusion, and to fostering social participation, integration and solidarity.*

With regard to what crime prevention means, what is required of it, what it can achieve, the 17th German Congress on Crime Prevent refers to the proceedings of the 12th,

13th, 14th, 15th and 16th German Congress on Crime Prevention, and to the calls and appeals contained in the Wiesbaden Declaration, the Leipzig Declaration, the Hanover Declaration, the Berlin Declaration, and the Oldenburg Declaration, whose validity and urgency remain in full force and effect.

Munich, 17 April 2012

Erich Marks / Marc Coester / Frederick Groeger-Roth / Burkhard Hasenpusch / Claudia Heinzelmann / Anja Meyer / Susanne Wolter[1]

Some experiences by the Crime Prevention Council of Lower Saxony (CPC) concerning quality-oriented and evidence-based prevention policies

Nowadays a quality-oriented and evidence-based approach is perceived essential for successful and effective crime-prevention. In this article we want to contribute a practical view to this mostly academic discussion. For a better understanding of some of the central developments in the interface of science, politics and practice we refer as an example to the experiences and working perspectives of the Crime Prevention Council of Lower Saxony (CPC).

1. Basic information of the Crime Prevention Council of Lower Saxony (CPC)

The Crime Prevention Council of Lower Saxony (CPC) was founded in 1995 on the basis of a resolution of the Lower-Saxony State Government. It is an independent advisory body of the government as well as of local committees and bodies in the field of the prevention.

Its primary goal is the reduction of crime in Lower Saxony and the improvement of the subjective feeling of security of the citizens of Lower Saxony. The Crime Prevention Council of Lower Saxony considers crime prevention as a task of society as a whole, strengthens crime prevention at the municipal level and coordinates and supports networking in crime prevention (see appendix 1: Objectives of the Crime Prevention Council of Lower Saxony).

Currently 15 employees with a wide spectrum of professional experiences and qualifications (social sciences, administration, social work, police, psychology, educational theory, sociology, criminal law, etc.) are working part and full time in the secretariat of the Crime Prevention Council of Lower Saxony.

Current activities of the CPC:

- Municipal Crime Prevention
- Prevention made to measure. CTC in Lower Saxony
- Prevention of Violence and Protection of Victims
- Prevention of Right-Wing Extremism
- Beccaria-Standards: Quality through Competence

---

[1] All members of the „working group for national and International networking" of the Crime Prevention Council of Lower Saxony (CPC)

- Co-operations in Lower Saxony
- National and international Networking

The secretariat is part of the Department of Justice. It develops concepts and coordinates sustainable crime-prevention strategies, necessary to obtain the objectives mentioned above. The secretariat works in accordance with the board of directors of the Crime Prevention Council which represents about 270 member organizations from all relevant social sectors. Besides approximately 200 local prevention bodies, non-governmental organizations, ministries and their subordinate agencies and academic institutions are among the member organizations. In more than 200 cities and communities in Lower Saxony so called local prevention bodies and networks contribute with their expertise to concepts concerning public security and support their realization. Supporting them and linking up their efforts is the primary task of the Crime Prevention Council of Lower Saxony (further information is provided on the websites of the CPC[2]).

2. Examples of efforts for quality-oriented and evidence-based prevention policies on federal state-level

The following concepts outline examples and approaches to a national Crime Prevention Policy that is more and more based on knowledge, quality management, effect orientation and systematic evaluation. This alignment of evidence-based crime prevention and criminal policy is characterized by a steady use of the current state of knowledge. The current projects and activities of the CPC have grown essentially in a pragmatic way, they are not yet based on an overall political strategy for a state-wide preventive action, an interdepartmental prevention plan. Department-bound individual decisions and conditions still have great influence on the actual prevention activities financed by different funding programs, for example at a national and European level. Furthermore, the cooperation between the key fields of work of prevention (prevention politics, prevention practice and prevention research) is still in the early stages of development.

2.1 Community coaching in a federal structure

The Lower Saxony Government stated in 1995, that in spite of a general decline of crime an „intensification of the crime-preventive efforts on local- and state level" was required. This development corresponded with the insight, that repressive measures alone have no sustainable effect on criminal activity. The demand for a „societal prevention" in Lower Saxony was formulated i.e. the cooperation of all departments as well as governmental and non-governmental organizations, who can contribute to prevention. As a consequence the CPC was founded.

---

[2] www.lpr.niedersachsen.de (german and english); www.beccaria.de (german); http://www.beccaria-standards.net (english and 18 other languages); www.beccaria-portal.org (english); www.gruene-liste-praevention.de (german)

The reasons for criminal behavior have to be sought primarily in the living environment of offenders. Crime prevention is primarily a community task, adequately supported by the state and regional actors. In this view, the principle of subsidiarity takes effect: tasks, actions and problem solutions ought to be handled by the smallest, lowest, or least centralized authority capable of addressing that matter effectively. Only if this isn't possible, gradually larger groups, public authorities or higher levels of an organization should have a subsidiary function. Related to crime prevention, this implies that primarily citizens, civil society organizations, municipalities, towns and administrative districts shall be responsible for crime prevention and then counties and federal states.

In Lower Saxony crime prevention is in the responsibility of communities, supported by the CPC when necessary. Local communities should be supported and advised to develop prevention bodies and practical structures in crime prevention. Out of this, the secretariat of the CPC has developed a model of intensive „on site-consulting", which led to a considerable increase in prevention bodies, especially in the 1990s. In 2000 the number of municipal prevention bodies supported by the CPC had tripled to a total of 99 (in 1995: 33) and a total of 138 in 2002. Since 2002 the CPC is also funding projects and supporting municipal prevention projects in Lower Saxony. Besides consultation, „support" was added as a further instrument.

Since then, the municipality as a field of action of societal prevention has gained significantly in importance. Currently 200 local prevention bodies and networks contribute with their expertise to concepts concerning public security and support their realization. Community prevention bodies are working on city level, in larger cities at the level of city districts, in collective municipalities, on municipal level as well as on state level. Many prevention bodies have been founded by a council order, several have originated from representatives of the police or youth welfare services and in some places from engaged citizens. Municipal prevention committees are characterized by a great variety of organizational forms and a big spectrum in the personal structure. Often prevention councils are connected to the administration, in this case often the mayor or district administrators are chairing the committee – according to the motto „prevention is a matter for the boss". The tie to the top management has turned out to be especially effective.

Due to the immediate and manifold communication between the different institutions – police, school, youth welfare service, justice – information and networking processes have been initiated, that lead to more acceptance of other professions and to an acceleration and simplifying of certain procedures.

The improvement of the dialogue and the cooperation between the actors is an important benefit of municipal crime prevention. Meanwhile we can find considerable qualitative changes in the daily working practice. Range, complexity and reach of the issues have become bigger and more varied since the origin of the first Lower Saxony committees in the early 1990s. Furthermore, there is an increasing public perception and acceptance concerning the work of the municipal prevention bodies.

Lower Saxony is a big state with approximately 1000 local authority districts. Concerning the number of committees there is still „place for more". Above all, especially in the rural areas, there is a lack of prevention committees. A proactive consultation approach or a big campaign, which cannot be performed due to financial reasons, would be necessary. Furthermore, up to now there are no available instruments to reach municipal top representatives, to make them act as a „door opener and key people for prevention" methodically and argumentatively. Besides, consultation approaches must be improved and diversified. It is obvious that directive consultations are often counterproductive for the individual actors and problem constellations on site. It makes sense besides the individualized consultation, to develop in the long term „tools" for „frequent problems and questions" in the area of local crime prevention, which can be used municipality wide.

A tool which points in this direction are the planning instruments for the municipal prevention strategy „CTC" (Communities That Care). This is suited for urban and rural areas. It is based on knowledge from scientific longitudinal research referring to risk- and protective factors and effective programs, but requires no scientific education of the users. The implementation quality of the method is the key. The meaning of quality management in municipal prevention has to be underlined.

2.2 Funding Program for Communal Crime Prevention

Since 2002 the CPC is funding crime prevention projects and scientific surveys especially on the municipal level. Numerous measures had been realized since then, primarily focused on children and juveniles. The funded projects as well as the funding guidelines were also evaluated. In particular with the priority program in 2013 and 2014 „Communities that Care - CTC" (see 2.9) the implementation of positively evaluated programs is promoted for the first time.

In future the funding program will support organizations and communities that perform their prevention work data based, quality-oriented, structured and willing to implement evidence-based programs. The respective programs and content priorities will not be predetermined by the CPC but rather should be based on scientific data collected on site.

2.3 Beccaria standards for ensuring quality in crime prevention projects

The Beccaria standards are named after Cesare Beccaria (1738-1794), the pioneer of modern crime policies. The Beccaria standards include measures and requirements for quality planning, execution and assessment of crime prevention programs and projects. They apply to the following seven key steps of a project:

1. Description of the problem
2. Analysis of the conditions leading to the emergence of the problem
3. Determination of prevention goals, project goals and targeted groups
4. Determining measures to achieve the objectives
5. Project design and implementation
6. Review of implementation and the achievement of its goals (evaluation)
7. Conclusion and documentation of the project

The Beccaria standards describe an overall program of requirements to ensure quality. A satisfactory guarantee for the quality of a project can only be achieved by complying with the overall program. The individual requirements are always in step with each other. Selective attention or inattention to particular steps of the Beccaria standards would be detrimental to the level of quality. The Beccaria standards offer a manual for developers, players in the field and other people with responsibility in crime prevention to ensure the quality of their crime prevention work. Whoever is responsible should ensure that

- they align the planning, implementation and review of crime prevention projects with the quality criteria outlined in science and literature,
- projects are designed in such a way that they can be evaluated,
- Scientific experts, advisors, contracting bodies and sponsors are at hand to provide a technical basis for judging the project's targeting of objectives and quality.

The standards are currently available online in different languages: Arabic, Chinese, Croatian, Czech, English, French, German, Hindi, Hungarian, Italian, Japanese, Korean, Lithuanian, Polish, Portuguese, Russian, Spanish, Swedish and Turkish. „Interactive Beccaria-Steps" as a special practice support lead online through all important questions in the process of project management. They are available in English and in German.

2.4 Beccaria Training Program

Since 2008 the Crime Prevention Council of Lower Saxony offers annually the „Beccaria Training Program Crime Prevention" to improve the quality of the work on site. The reason for the design and implementation was the increasing demand for interdisciplinary prevention training. The modular qualification „Crime Prevention

Specialist" is aimed at all those working in crime prevention that wants to expand their knowledge of criminology, crime prevention and project management. The Qualification Program comprises four key modules: Criminology, Crime Prevention, Project Management and Practical Project Work.

The contents are application-oriented and based on scientific evidence. The knowledge acquired is directly applicable to daily prevention work. Upon completion, participants are qualified to evaluate criminological theories and empirical studies, to plan, implement and review crime prevention projects according to the quality criteria outlined in science and literature, to apply methods of project management and to use the knowledge (criminological, crime preventive) acquired in daily practice. The standard period of study for the qualification program is one year. Every module is spread out over two weekends. The qualification is designed as an in-service training and limited to a number of 25 participants per module. Upon successful completion of the four modules, the degree „Crime Prevention Specialist" is awarded. Currently there are a total of 120 specialists. The „Beccaria Training Program Crime Prevention" was externally evaluated in 2012.

2.5 Further qualification offers and perspective for a Beccaria Academy

The CPC provides with his professional advanced training topical and interdisciplinary knowledge and educates further actors need- and work-oriented. The following qualification offers count to the modular qualification measures: The „Beccaria-Training Program Crime Prevention", the „Qualification victims counseling in the field of right wing extremism", the education „certified trainer in the method Communities That Care - CTC". In addition, the CPC regularly designs practice seminars and training series on various prevention topics. The long term goal is to build a Beccaria Academy under the leadership of the CPC.

2.6 Beccaria-Master and perspective for an advanced master study program

In 2011 the Ostfalia-University of Applied Sciences in Wolfenbüttel started the consecutive Master's program „Preventive Social Work focusing on criminology & crime prevention". The concept for the program emerged from the „Beccaria Project: Professional Training in crime prevention" of the CPC. The advanced study program (standard period of four semesters) is addressed to persons aspiring to executive positions in fields related to crime prevention. The educational and admission requirements include a degree in Social Work or comparable courses and work experience in a related field. According to the understanding of prevention as a societal crosscutting issue the course is designed interdisciplinary. A targeted goal is to offer an application oriented study program „Crime Prevention" in form of Distance Learning, Massive Open Online Courses (MOOC) or Blended Learning, didactically useful attendance courses combined with virtual learning on the basis of new information and communication media.

2.7 Regional analysis and audit guidelines

Criminological regional analysis (CRA) and local audits are intended to provide local prevention bodies and stakeholders a data base for planning prevention activities. CRA usually consists of a small region analysis of the data from the police crime statistics and a survey of the population about their victimization and/or fear of crime. So far only ten municipalities in Lower Saxony have performed such analysis. Moreover, it is usually a „one shot"-activity carried out only once. Very few municipalities use CRA as a regular instrument. In many cases it seems to be unclear how significant the data collected are for the specific project planning. For a good profit of local audits it is necessary that reliable data analysis, systematic implementation and final evaluation are carried out regularly.

Since 2013, due to its membership in the German-European Forum for Urban Security (DEFUS), the CPC is involved in a triennial EU project focusing on the improvement of safety audit processes. In this project an overview of existing methods will be developed, best practice procedures are sought all over Europe and a handbook with recommendations is planned. A manual of the European Forum for Urban Safety (EFUS) that was translated into German in 2007 by the CPC can be used for this project.

2.8 Systematic state-wide data processing in preparation

To support the Lower Saxony municipalities in crime prevention, relevant data sets should be presented and interpreted in their scope and meaning. In the long term, an annual small-scale monitoring of crime prevention in Lower Saxony is intended. This would include the presentation of current, valid and small-scale data that represent the starting point for crime and violence prevention measures in Lower Saxony and which can be analyzed according to positive changes after implementing measures.

A first inventory is being started. The targeted „data monitor" refers to the crime rate of the population and their subjective sense of security, i.e. to the base-line, which is not yet sufficiently systematically collected and documented in the prevention activities of the Lower Saxony communities. This „data monitor " cannot provide a complete and clear picture, but will have many blind spots. It should show what data – ideally regularly updated – are available where. In addition, it is supposed to represent what data should be included in a regular preventive monitoring.

2.9 Model Project SPIN and state-wide rollout of „CTC – Prevention made to measure"

In the pilot project (SPIN: 2009 - 2012), the CPC has adapted and implemented the method developed in the USA „Communities That Care - CTC" for the first time in the German-speaking world. The goal was to provide the municipalities and the municipal bodies an evidence-based planning tool for prevention. In the pilot phase, CTC could be implemented successfully in the three pilot sites in Lower Saxony. As a result of the pilot project, CPC is now offering CTC to all interested municipalities in Lower Saxony. With the beginning of 2013, six new sites in Lower Saxony are implementing CTC. A state-wide survey with the CTC-Youth Survey in 2013 provides representative data on the extent of problem behavior of youth and about their exposure to risk or protective factors.

2.10 Green List Prevention

In Germany plenty of prevention programs are on the market. Within the CTC pilot project the CPC developed a recommendation list of evaluated prevention programs, primarily to allow CTC users to select suitable measures to develop local action plans.

The „Green List Prevention" reflects the status of the development of selected program approaches as precisely as possible. Therefore, the recommended prevention programs are divided into three stages with respect to the evidence of effectiveness: (1) effectiveness theoretically plausible, (2) effectiveness likely, and (3) effectiveness proven.

A status „on the threshold" is reached if not all criteria for the level for a theoretically convincing model are fulfilled, i.e. if necessary information for classification is not available or no evaluation was made. The database „Green List Prevention" allows specific searching criteria, such as the targeted risk and protective factors, the problem behaviors prevented by the programs, the age of the target groups, or the operational area in order to promote a further development of local supply structures.

The database „Green List Prevention" is available online and contains a unique overview of evaluated prevention programs, differentiated by a transparent evaluation system. A regular platform with the recommended programs has been established. There is a strong demand from practice for the „Green List Prevention" beyond CTC. Therefore an expansion is planned to include additional fields of prevention (e.g. indicated programs) and an extension of the scoring system to aspects of the implementation quality of programs.

2.11 Cooperation in the field of prevention research

The CPC has adopted the goal to promote the transfer of knowledge in crime prevention by initiating its own research projects, or through collaborations with research institutions. Currently, for example, there is collaboration with the University of Hildesheim (Institute of Psychology) for further development and use of the CTC - Youth Survey (see above). Based on the results of the state-wide CTC - Youth Survey further research questions should be developed and processed. For the future it is planned to expand the cooperation in the field of prevention research. There are regular contacts at the national and international level, for example, to the Society for Prevention Research (SPR) and the European Society for Prevention Research.

2.12 Development of QM-strategies

From 2013 the work area „prevention of right wing extremism" and in particular the Experts-network (a state-wide association of approximately 60 persons and institutions working in the field against right wing extremism) are certified according to the „customer focused quality of counseling organizations (KQB)". KQB is a method for quality development and has its starting and reference point in the specific consultation process. In the coming years, all counseling services are performed according to audited standards, reflected, monitored and evaluated.

In addition to the „quality testing for consulting organizations (KQB)" the CPC aims at an external quality attestation of CPC educational opportunities in the long term. Caused by the „KQB process" the quality of the overall design of the CPC trainings is checked and certified by an independent, neutral body.

2.13 Project CTC Europe

With the start of the CTC-pilot project the CPC also has encouraged a regular exchange of information with the other European CTC-users and researchers. So far, the networking at the international level was limited to the exchange of experience, apart from individual bilateral research projects (USA – Australia, USA – The Netherlands). For the years 2013-2015 the European network receives an EU project funding by the ISEC Programme (the project partners come from the following countries: Germany, Great Britain, Croatia, the Netherlands, Austria, Sweden and Cyprus). The CTC – EU project aims are:

- transnational comparison of the results of the CTC-Youth Surveys,
- the development of an European database of effective prevention programs,
- a transnational comparison of CTC-evaluation studies with the aim of developing a European CTC-implementation manual.

2.14 Collaborations at the national and international level

For an up-to-date work in the field of crime prevention, it is essential to establish, evaluate and to expand contacts with other stakeholders in this field. Since 2008 the working group „National and international Networks" is meeting once a week. It looks systematically at the work of the CPC and maintains existing national and international contacts. The participation of its members in conferences and congresses is planned and analyzed there. The participation of the CPC in projects and programs of different national and international partners is coordinated as well as the acquisition of third-party funding at national and international level. Moreover, this working group discusses cross-project issues and current developments relevant for prevention. Planned are a targeted analysis of the „environment" of national and international stakeholders and the establishment of additional contacts in close-by fields of prevention.

2.15 Evaluations of own measures

The CPC understands evaluation as a mandate to describe all areas of work with appropriate empirical methods, to analyze, to evaluate and to derive improvement and processes of change. This basic understanding also will refer to the organization of conferences, advanced training and training programs, (pilot) projects, studies, funding programs and all other working areas.

2.16 Acceptance of other areas in evidence-based prevention strategies

The section „prevention of right wing extremism" is currently implementing state-level and federal programs. They inform and prime on one side (target group is interested) and on the other side they help and give advice in problem situations (target group is affected). In the future, if the mandate is formulated for this purpose, primary and secondary or universal, selective and indicated evidence-based prevention programs could be implemented exemplarily in the field of the development of prejudice and the inclination to aggression (as at least two of the major theoretical explanations of right wing extremism) in relevant locations.

2.17 National project- database NiMaP

The NiMaP database (Lower Saxony measures of prevention) was developed in 2010 under the aegis of the CPC in cooperation with the Ministries of Social Affairs, Justice, of Internal Affairs, of Education and the Prime Minister's Office. It is a system for the electronic management and selective research of specific data, concerning specific measures and projects of Lower Saxony in the fields of violence prevention, crime prevention, drug prevention, child and youth protection, and prevention against extremism.

The database provides to the public at large a comfortable and extensive research opportunity for activities and projects of Lower Saxony. Perspectively other areas of prevention should be included in this database. Also, the existing information base should be better used for a continuous and regular exchange among ministries. In view of current and planned measures, the database should be used more for networking and cooperation between the departments in an efficient, resource-saving and interdisciplinary prevention work of Lower Saxony.

The findings on the overall situation of available measures should lead to a lively exchange of departments regarding requirements, parallel structures and redundancy. As a result, resources could be better targeted. The cash flow is determined by the state-level data available. This would be to identify in advance a comprehensive „prevention-oriented picture" of the situation.

3. Appraisals and recommendations

Prevention Politics, Prevention Practice and Prevention Research can be seen as the central focus areas of a holistic and sustainable orientation in prevention. Perspectively and for all three fields of work similarly these three areas have to be considered holistically and not limited to the sections of crime prevention, addiction prevention, poverty prevention or disease prevention, for example. The necessity of a structured and intensive cooperation of these three areas of work should be at least carried out at the levels of the communities/regions, at the national/ state level as well as at the international/global level. Multi-disciplinarity, profile formation and information are such indispensable tasks and qualities for each of the three prevention fields.

The following diagram represents an ideal model of the interdependencies and network formations on the one hand as well as of the regional, national and international levels on the other hand between the areas of prevention politics, prevention practice and prevention research.

In particular the profiles of these three areas of work should be communicated more actively. Every area of work should communicate its profile clearly with a high degree of general intelligibility as well as freely accessible.

Diagram: Ideal model of the interdependencies in prevention

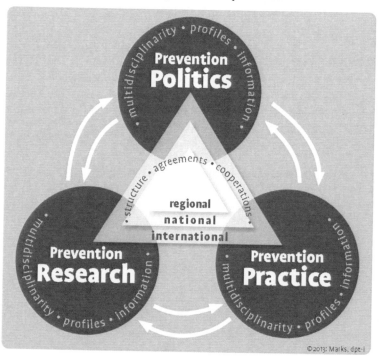

Multidisciplinarity

Multidisciplinary collaboration should be systematically organized and guaranteed in every field of prevention work. In the field of work „prevention politics" representatives of political parties, the legislative, the various departments of the executive and the judiciary should be involved. In the field of work „prevention practice" representatives of youth, education, health and social services, the police, non-governmental and voluntary organizations should be represented. Within the field of work of „prevention research" public, government and private research institutions with relevant disciplines and sub-disciplines (e.g., sociology, psychology, biology, medicine, political science, law, economics, criminology, victimology, etc.) should also be involved as well as research funding organizations and scientific associations.

Profiles

An important requirement for a successful societal prevention orientation is a clear self-conception of the individual fields of work. Definitional requirements, self-conception and responsibilities should be formulated by prevention politics, prevention practice and prevention research. To clarify profiles and portfolios in each of the three areas of work clear descriptions of the existing resources, capacity and structured offers are required.

Information Policy

In particular, the profiles of the work of prevention politics, prevention practice and prevention research should be communicated in future more actively. Each work area should make their profile proactive easily accessible with a high degree of comprehensibility.

Structure

On the three key levels of communication, the local/regional level, the state/national level and the international/global level; prevention politics, prevention practice, and prevention research should equally cooperate in permanent structures and possibly include also other partner organizations. In such permanent structures mutual information, basic agreements and concrete cooperation could be implemented transparently and sustainably.

Agreements

Besides an efficient communication within and between the respective fields of prevention and prevention levels, it becomes increasingly important to agree on terms, definitions, objectives, criteria, methods, different profiles and responsibilities and priorities, strategies and specific projects and programs.

Cooperations

Through a formalized and consistent communication between the areas prevention politics, prevention practice and prevention research joint positions could be published, concrete project proposals prepared, implemented and evaluated.

Besides the subject-specific methodological responses from the respective views of the participating disciplines and prevention stakeholders, more fundamental and extensive structural changes are needed, if prevention and intervention measures are to be effectively and successfully developed, implemented and evaluated. Crucial is a new culture of communication between the three fields of prevention politics, prevention practice and prevention research which are highly dependent on each other.

Appendix: Objectives

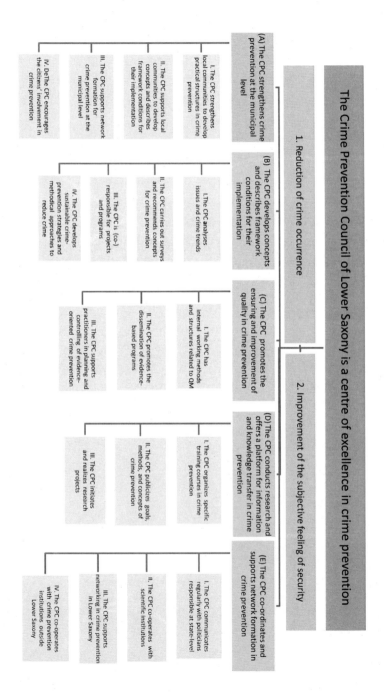

Program of the 6th Annual International Forum

Monday, 16. April 2012

11:00 - 12:30 - Hall 1
Opening Plenum of the German Congress on Crime Prevention
(German with interpretation into English)

- Welcome by the Executive Director of the German Congress on Crime Prevention
  Erich Marks, German Congress on Crime Prevention
- Welcoming address
  Christian Ude, Lord Mayor of the City of Munich
- Welcoming address
  Joachim Hermann, Minister of the Interior of the Federal State of Bavaria
- Welcoming address
  Professor Dr. Hans-Jürgen Kerner, President of the German Foundation for Crime Prevention and Assistance of Criminal Offenders
- Remarks about the main topic of the congress
  Dr. Wiebke Steffen, Author of the Report for the Congress
- Welcoming address
  Guilherme Pinto, President of the European Forum for Urban Security
- Welcoming address
  Professor Gerd Neubeck, Director for Security Deutsche Bahn AG
- Keynote Speech "Balanced Investing in Proven Crime Prevention: A Crime Victim Right"
  Professor Dr. Irvin Waller, University of Ottawa

12:30 - 14:00
Luncheon for international guests

14:00 - 15:00 - Hall 12b
Sustaining and Mainstreaming Pre-crime Prevention: Glasgow, Bogotá and Alberta
Prof. Dr. Irvin Waller, University of Ottawa, Canada

Chair: Dr. Marc Coester (German Congress on Crime Prevention) and Dr. Burkhard Hasenpusch (Crime Prevention Council Lower Saxony)

15:30 - 16:30 - Hall 12b
Engaging young people in designing against crime
Dr. Caroline L. Davey and Andrew B. Wootton, University of Salford, United Kingdom

Chair: Dr. Burkhard Hasenpusch (Crime Prevention Council Lower Saxony)

17:00 - 18:00 - Hall 4b
Presentation of the International Report on Crime Prevention and Community Safety 2012
Dr. Paula Miraglia, International Centre for the Prevention of Crime ICPC, Canada

Chair: Dr. Marc Coester (German Congress on Crime Prevention) and Johannes de Haan
(United Nations Office on Drugs and Crime)

18:15 - 20:00 - ICM Foyer (upper floor)
Evening Reception of the German Congress on Crime Prevention

Tuesday, 17. April 2012

09:00 - 10:00 - Hall 12b
Sexual Harassment, Sexual Assault and Women's Right to the City: Lessons from the Gender Inclusive Cities Programme
Dr. Sohail Husain, Analytica Consulting, Hampshire, United Kingdom

Chair: Dr. Burkhard Hasenpusch (Crime Prevention Council Lower Saxony)

10:30 - 11:30 - Hall 12b
Building Safer and Gender Inclusive Cities: The Experience of Delhi
Kalpana Viswanath, Delhi, India

Chair: Juma Assiago (UN-HABITAT)

11:30 - 12:30 - Catering Area - Opportunity for Lunch

12:30 - 13:30 - Hall 12b
Violence Prevention: Experiences from South Africa
Dr. Tina Silbernagl, GIZ South Africa and Partners from South Africa

Chair: Dr. Rainer Strobl (proVal Institute)

14:00 - 15:00 - Hall 12b
Preventing violence: an overview
Dr. Alexander Butchart, World Health Organization (WHO), Switzerland

Chair: Dr. Burkhard Hasenpusch (Crime Prevention Council Lower Saxony)

15:00 - 16:00 - Hall 1
Closing Plenum of the German Congress on Crime Prevention
(German with interpretation into English)

The „Munich Declaration" from the German Congress on Crime Prevention
Dr. Wiebke Steffen, Author of the Report for the Congress

Closing Remarks
Prof. Dr. Hans-Jürgen Kerner, Congress President

„Roads of the Security Society"
Prof. Dr. Axel Groenemeyer, University of Dortmund

Outlook and closing address
Erich Marks, Executive Director of the German Congress on Crime Prevention

Authors

Dr. Alexander Butchart
World Health Organization (WHO), Switzerland

Dr. Marc Coester
Crime Prevention Council of Lower Saxony (CPC), Germany

Dr. Caroline L. Davey
University of Salford, United Kingdom

Frederick Groeger-Roth
Crime Prevention Council of Lower Saxony (CPC), Germany

Dr. Burkhard Hasenpusch
Crime Prevention Council of Lower Saxony (CPC), Germany

Dr. Claudia Heinzelmann
Crime Prevention Council of Lower Saxony (CPC), Germany

Philipp Kuehl
Deutsche Gesellschaft für Internationale Zusammenarbeit (GIZ), Germany

Erich Marks
German Congress on Crime Prevention, Hannover, Germany

Melissa Marselle
University of Salford, United Kingdom

Dr. Anja Meyer
Crime Prevention Council of Lower Saxony (CPC), Germany

Dr. Tina Silbernagl
Deutsche Gesellschaft für Internationale Zusammenarbeit (GIZ), Germany

Prof. Dr. Irvin Waller
University of Ottawa, Canada

Susanne Wolter
Crime Prevention Council of Lower Saxony (CPC), Germany

Andrew B. Wootton
University of Salford, United Kingdom